Raising Money for Education

Raising Money for Education

A Guide to the Property Tax

David H. Monk
Brian O. Brent

CORWIN PRESS, INC.
A Sage Publications Company
Thousand Oaks, California

For information:

Corwin Press, Inc.
A Sage Publications Company
2455 Teller Road
Thousand Oaks, California 91320
E-mail: order@corwin.sagepub.com

SAGE Publications Ltd.
6 Bonhill Street
London EC2A 4PU
United Kingdom

SAGE Publications India Pvt. Ltd.
M-32 Market
Greater Kailash I
New Delhi 110 048 India

Printed in the United States of America

Library of Congress Cataloging-in-Publication Data

Monk, David H.
　Raising money for education: A guide to the property
tax / by David H. Monk and Brian O. Brent.
　　p. cm.
　Includes bibliographical references and index.
　ISBN 0-8039-6406-4 (cloth: acid-free paper). — ISBN
0-8039-6407-2 (pbk.: acid-free paper)
　　1. Education—United States—Finance. 2. Property tax—United
States. I. Brent, Brian O. II. Title.
　LB2825.M534 1997
　379.1'3—dc21　　　　　　　　　　　　　　　　　　97-4885

97　98　99　00　01　02　03　10　9　8　7　6　5　4　3　2　1

Editorial Assistant: Kristen L. Gibson
Production Editor: Michele Lingre
Production Assistant: Lynn Miyata
Typesetter/Designer: Rebecca Evans
Indexer: Teri Greenberg
Cover Designer: Marcia M. Rosenburg

CONTENTS

PREFACE

BASEBALL, APPLE PIE, AND THE PROPERTY TAX

Soon after the colonists set foot on New England soil, taxes on property were levied and collected. However steeped in American tradition, the cry of baseball, apple pie, and the property tax is rarely heard. In fact, when asked "Which tax do you think is the worst tax?" respondents consistently identify the property tax as the least desirable. Despite its lack of public appeal, the property tax remains the primary source of revenues for local governments, including school districts.

There is, however, increasing awareness of a need to make changes in how revenues are raised for public schools, particularly property taxes. Since 1990, more than half the states have been involved in litigation addressing the financing of public education, many of which reviewed the use of the real property tax as a major source of local revenues. A school finance system that is dependent on the property wealth of a district is alleged to permit wide disparities in spending, which in turn foster inequities in educational opportunities and tax burdens across communities. In response to these challenges, several states, most notably Michigan and Texas, have implemented far-reaching reforms.

Politicians and local taxpayers have also entered the fray. The 1994 elections saw no fewer than 14 states with ballot propositions that dealt with school revenue issues. Judging from school budget defeats alone, voters also appear to be venting their frustrations over property tax increases. In fact, in the 1990s, approximately one third of school districts had their initial proposed budgets defeated in referenda, nearly double the figures reported in the 1980s. Forfeitures on the payment of school property taxes, termed *arrearages*, have also increased dramatically in the past decade.

In short, there is a growing sense that education policymakers need to become more sensitive to the inequities and inefficiencies associated with the generation of local resources for education, particularly the property tax. These are pressing concerns, given the increase in education spending in recent years. The purpose of this book is to provide insight into issues surrounding the generation of local revenues for public education in general and the property tax in particular.

Chapter 1 begins by providing an overview of recent trends in revenue sources for public schools. This review points to a shift in primary funding responsibility from state to local governments, typically school districts. The chapter also highlights the growing dependency of local districts on property tax revenues. The next two chapters examine attributes that should be considered when assessing the merits and shortcomings of a given tax for purposes of financing education. Chapter 2 looks to theories of taxation to uncover the elements that should be present if a tax system is to treat taxpayers fairly or equitably. Chapter 3 expands on these equity notions and introduces a framework for evaluating the desirability of various education taxes.

Next, Chapter 4 examines how the property tax system operates. The mechanics of the property tax is the essential starting point for understanding current efforts at local education finance reform, and this discussion sets the stage for the remaining chapters in the book. Chapter 5 explores a number of alternative property tax reforms. The presumption is that although the property tax has problems, it is still an appropriate mechanism for supporting public education that can be made to function more effectively through reforms of its structure and administration. In Chapter 6, the proposition is that the property tax's shortcomings warrant a shift away from its use. There, the focus is on alternatives that move away from the property tax, such as taxes based on either income or sales and lotteries. Chapter 7 examines the use of nontraditional revenue sources, such as user fees and donations. The presumption in Chapter 7 is that the use of these alternative revenue sources can allow districts to decrease their reliance on the local property tax. Last, Chapter 8 concludes with our final comments and recommendations for generating local dollars for education.

About the Authors

Brian O. Brent is Assistant Professor of Educational Administration in the Warner School of Education and Human Development at the University of Rochester. He earned his doctorate at Cornell University. He is a Certified Public Accountant who also holds a master's degree in taxation from Arizona State University. He is interested in revenue issues of public school finance and taxpayer equity.

David H. Monk is Chair of the Department of Education and Professor of Educational Administration at Cornell University. He earned his doctorate at the University of Chicago and has taught in a visiting capacity at the University of Rochester and the University of Burgundy in Dijon, France. He is author of *Educational Finance: An Economic Approach* as well as numerous articles in scholarly journals. He serves on the editorial boards of *The Economics of Education Review, The Journal of Educational Finance, Educational Policy* and *The Journal of Research in Rural Education* and recently chaired the technical study group appointed by the New York State Board of Regents to examine alternative revenue sources for New York public schools.

ONE

WHERE DOES THE MONEY COME FROM?

Funding for public education requires large amounts of money. In 1994-1995, approximately $268 billion dollars were raised for public elementary and secondary education, an increase of $170 billion since 1980. The increase in total *actual* education dollars has prompted widespread concern in recent years that schools are using resources inefficiently. Although this may prove true in certain cases, the actual figures reported in Table 1.1 need to be viewed in light of several factors that have contributed to the growth in school revenues. First, education spending is likely to increase as a result of inflation. Indeed, schools not only face increases in the costs of supplies and equipment, but more important, they must continually increase salaries to keep pace with shifts in the economy. The fourth column of Table 1.1 presents total education revenues adjusted for inflation (in 1987 dollars).

When expressed in inflation-adjusted dollars, the amount of total education revenue still increased during the period but at a much slower rate.

In addition to inflation, changes in the number of students also affects schools' demand for revenues. Table 1.1 reveals that the number of students enrolled in public schools increased overall throughout the 1980s and early 1990s. These figures suggest that at least a portion of the increase in revenues during the period were used to meet the needs of the increased student body.

Table 1.2 reports figures that account for changes in revenue levels that can be attributed to inflation and shifts in student enrollments.

TABLE 1.1 School Revenue Summary, 1979-1980 to 1994-1995

Year	Number of Students	Total Revenue in Actual Dollars (in millions)	Total Revenue in Inflation-Adjusted Dollars (in millions)[a]
1979-1980	41,651	97,635	144,004
1980-1981	40,877	106,553	144,185
1981-1982	40,044	113,998	143,937
1982-1983	39,566	120,485	144,380
1983-1984	39,252	128,875	147,623
1984-1985	39,208	141,013	154,281
1985-1986	39,422	153,807	162,073
1986-1987	39,753	163,767	166,769
1987-1988	40,008	176,266	172,556
1988-1989	40,189	193,234	181,526
1989-1990	40,543	208,656	188,148
1990-1991	41,217	223,896	194,608
1991-1992	42,047	234,923	198,247
1992-1993	42,735	247,436	203,567
1993-1994	43,353	255,769	205,354
1994-1995	44,237	267,749	210,082

SOURCE: Adapted from Center for the Study of States (1995), Public School Finance Programs of the United States and Canada, 1993-1994, Table 3.

a. Figures are expressed in 1987 dollars.

The table suggests that even after adjusting for these factors, revenues for education increased approximately 37% since 1980. Table 1.2 not only points to an increase in education spending in the past 15 years but also to a dramatic shift in the responsibility for public education among the levels of government. For example, the state share of education spending has declined steadily since the mid-1980s, whereas the local share has increased during the same period. Table 1.3 restates these figures in percentage terms.

The figures reported in these tables reveal national trends in how revenues are raised for elementary and secondary education. Table

TABLE 1.2 Inflation-Adjusted Revenue Per Pupil, 1979-1980 to 1994-1995

Year	Number of Students	Total Revenue in Inflation-Adjusted Dollars (in millions)[a]	Total	Federal	State	Local
1979-1980	41,651	144,004	3,457	319	1,697	1,441
1980-1981	40,877	144,185	3,527	307	1,701	1,519
1981-1982	40,044	143,937	3,594	265	1,721	1,608
1982-1983	39,566	144,380	3,649	263	1,740	1,646
1983-1984	39,252	147,623	3,761	263	1,798	1,700
1984-1985	39,208	154,281	3,935	266	1,928	1,741
1985-1986	39,422	162,073	4,111	277	2,030	1,805
1986-1987	39,753	166,769	4,195	270	2,089	1,836
1987-1988	40,008	172,556	4,313	277	2,126	1,911
1988-1989	40,189	181,526	4,517	288	2,192	2,036
1989-1990	40,543	188,148	4,641	293	2,242	2,106
1990-1991	41,217	194,608	4,722	299	2,278	2,145
1991-1992	42,047	198,247	4,715	315	2,235	2,165
1992-1993	42,735	203,567	4,763	332	2,230	2,201
1993-1994	43,353	205,354	4,737	341	2,179	2,217
1994-1995	44,237	210,082	4,749	347	2,183	2,218

SOURCE: Adapted from Center for the Study of States (1995), Public School Finance Programs of the United States and Canada, 1993-1994, Table 3.

a. Figures are expressed in 1987 dollars.

1.4 presents the composition of school revenues for the 50 states and the District of Columbia for years 1986-1987, 1989-1990, 1993-1994.

As Table 1.4 makes clear, the primary responsibility for funding schools varies considerably across the states. For example, Hawaii derives approximately 91% of school revenues from state sources. In contrast, New Hampshire's local share accounts for almost 89% of all school revenues.

On average, state revenues are raised from the following taxes: sales tax (32.8%), personal income tax (31.8%), corporate income tax

TABLE 1.3 Inflation-Adjusted Revenue Per Pupil, Percentage
by Source, 1979-1980 to 1994-1995

Year	Number of Students	Total Revenue in Inflation-Adjusted Dollars (in millions)[a]	Federal %	State %	Local %
1979-1980	41,651	144,004	9.24	49.09	41.67
1980-1981	40,877	144,185	8.71	48.22	43.07
1981-1982	40,044	143,937	7.39	48.02	44.74
1982-1983	39,566	144,380	7.21	47.68	45.11
1983-1984	39,252	147,623	6.99	47.81	45.21
1984-1985	39,208	154,281	6.76	49.01	44.23
1985-1986	39,422	162,073	6.73	49.37	43.90
1986-1987	39,753	166,769	6.44	49.79	43.76
1987-1988	40,008	172,556	6.42	49.28	44.30
1988-1989	40,189	181,526	6.3	48.54	45.07
1989-1990	40,543	188,148	6.32	48.30	45.38
1990-1991	41,217	194,608	6.33	48.25	45.42
1991-1992	42,047	198,247	6.68	47.40	45.92
1992-1993	42,735	203,567	6.97	46.82	46.21
1993-1994	43,353	205,354	7.20	46.00	46.80
1994-1995	44,237	210,082	7.32	45.97	46.71

SOURCE: Adapted from Center for the Study of States (1995), Public School
Finance Programs of the United States and Canada, 1993-1994, Table 3.
a. Figures are expressed in 1987 dollars.

(6.6%), and excise taxes (16.7%) (Center for the Study of States, 1995).
Whereas the state share is derived from a variety of tax mechanisms,
the local share is secured almost entirely from the property tax. In
fact, in 1991, there were only four states where the property tax ac-
counted for less than 98% of the local tax revenue of school districts:[1]

- Louisiana derived 57% of local revenues from a local sales tax,
  with 43% from the property tax.
- Kentucky derived 67% of local revenues from the property
  tax, with 13.6% from local income taxes and 19.4% from other
  local taxes.

TABLE 1.4 Level and Composition of School Revenue by State (in percentages)

State	1986-1987			1989-1990			1993-1994		
	Federal	State	Local	Federal	State	Local	Federal	State	Local
United States	6.44	49.79	43.76	6.32	48.3	45.38	7.2	46.0	46.8
Alabama	11.80	66.5	21.6	13.50	67.10	19.40	13.1	65.4	21.6
Alaska	10.20	68.9	20.9	9.90	60.50	29.60	12.60	63.6	23.8
Arizona	8.90	57	34.2	4.70	45.10	50.20	8.90	42.3	48.9
Arkansas	11.40	56.6	32	9.70	59.50	30.80	9.40	63.1	27.5
California	7.30	68.9	23.8	8	66.80	25.10	8.90	54.9	36.2
Colorado	4.90	38.9	56.2	4.80	38.10	57	5.80	46	48.2
Connecticut	3.50	40.2	56.3	3.70	44.70	51.60	4.60	39.5	55.9
Delaware	8.10	68.8	23.1	7.90	66.80	25.30	9.10	65.1	25.8
District of Columbia	10.90	NA	89.1	10.10	NA	89.90	NA	NA	NA
Florida	7.60	54	38.4	6	53.60	40.50	7.70	49.8	42.4
Georgia	8.20	57.1	34.7	6.50	60.90	32.60	8.40	49.4	42.2
Hawaii	10.50	89.4	0.1	7.90	92	0.10	7.10	90.9	2.1
Idaho	9.50	57.4	33.1	7.20	59.90	32.90	8.10	60.9	30.9
Illinois	4.60	38.5	56.9	7.70	37.90	54.40	8.20	32.9	58.8
Indiana	4.80	57.6	37.5	4.50	59.20	36.20	5.20	52.1	42.6
Iowa	5.20	43.1	51.7	5.30	51.00	43.70	5.70	48.4	45.9

continued

TABLE 1.4 continued

State	1986-1987			1989-1990			1993-1994		
	Federal	State	Local	Federal	State	Local	Federal	State	Local
Kansas	4.80	44.1	51	5.20	43.30	51.50	5.50	49.7	44.9
Kentucky	13.30	63	23.6	9.20	69.70	21.10	10.20	67.2	22.6
Louisiana	10.60	54.7	34.7	11.30	54.40	34.30	12.30	53.6	34.0
Maine	6.20	50.1	43.7	6.70	53.20	40.10	7	48.5	44.4
Maryland	5.40	38.9	55.7	4.90	38.70	56.30	5.60	39	55.4
Massachusetts	5	41.7	53.2	4.40	42.40	53.20	5.50	36	58.5
Michigan	5.90	34.9	59.3	4.70	36.30	59.00	5.70	32.1	62.2
Minnesota	4.30	55.7	40.1	4.40	53.20	42.40	5.10	46.5	48.5
Mississippi	12	64.7	23.3	15.50	56.70	27.80	16.6	53.8	29.6
Missouri	6.5	54.7	52.9	5.60	38	56.40	6.6	37.5	55.9
Montana	7	49	44	8	47.7	44.3	9.2	53.8	37.0
Nebraska	6.50	24.3	69.3	4.80	24.30	70.80	4.80	39.1	56.1
Nevada	5	46.9	48.2	4.10	26.70	59.30	5	36	59.0
New Hampshire	4.20	6.9	88.9	2.70	7.80	89.60	2.80	8.3	88.9
New Jersey	4.80	44.2	51	3.80	41.50	54.70	4.20	41.5	54.3
New Mexico	12.40	75.4	12.2	12	76.4	11.6	10.3	61.8	27.9
New York	5.70	41.1	53.2	5	43.40	51.70	5.60	39.2	55.2
North Carolina	8.80	66.2	25	6.30	65.70	27.90	8.90	63.8	27.3

North Dakota	8.90	53.1	38.1	7.00	49.70	43.30	11.50	43.6	44.9
Ohio	5.70	45.6	48.8	5.40	47.10	47.50	6.20	43.4	50.4
Oklahoma	5.90	63.3	30.9	8.7	59.1	32.2	7.4	63.3	29.4
Oregon	6.6	28.5	64.9	6.3	26.8	66.9	7.3	41	51.7
Pennsylvania	5.40	45.5	49.1	5.30	45.90	48.90	6.20	41.4	52.5
Rhode Island	4.90	41.1	54	4.40	43.80	51.80	4.50	40.7	54.8
South Carolina	9.30	57.8	32.9	7.70	53.30	39.00	9.60	46.9	43.5
South Dakota	12.10	27.4	60.6	9.30	27.30	63.40	10.80	25.3	63.9
Tennessee	12.20	42.6	45.2	9.40	48.30	42.40	9.80	48.9	41.3
Texas	7.40	47.6	45.1	7.90	43.10	48.90	8.50	43.4	48.1
Utah	5.70	55.6	38.7	6.30	56.70	37.00	7.10	54.9	38.0
Vermont	5.80	32.4	61.8	5.30	36.50	58.20	5.20	32.4	62.5
Virginia	NA	NA	NA	4.70	34.70	60.60	6.60	34.2	59.2
Washington	6.10	74.1	19.8	5.80	73.40	20.80	5.90	71	23.0
West Virginia	7.90	68.4	23.7	8.20	64.30	27.50	8.20	64.6	27.2
Wisconsin	4.80	36.6	58.7	4.10	39.10	56.80	4.40	38.7	56.9
Wyoming	3.60	37.7	58.6	4.50	56.80	38.80	5.80	52.2	42.1

SOURCE: Adapted from Center for the Study of States (1995), Public School Finance Programs of the United States and Canada, 1993-94, Table 4.2; National Education Association, Estimates of School Statistics, 1989-90.

- Pennsylvania derived 83.8% of local revenues from the property tax, with 9.3% from local income taxes.
- South Dakota derived 95.9% of local revenues from the property tax, with 3.0% from local income taxes.

In addition to those in Kentucky and Pennsylvania, school districts in Iowa and Ohio collect local income taxes; however, they compose less than 1% of total local revenues.

Two observations follow from this discussion. First, many states have shifted funding responsibility for schools from the state to the local level. Second, increases in the local share mean increases in the property tax. Therefore, policymakers interested in altering the mix of education revenues would be wise to focus attention on local revenue sources in general and the property tax in particular.

Final Comments

This chapter provided a brief overview of changes in school revenue patterns during the past two decades. Readers interested in more detailed descriptions of school-funding systems are encouraged to consult *Public School Finance Programs of the United States and Canada 1993-94, Volumes 1-2* (Center for the Study of States, 1995).

Note

1. Figures for 1991 are the latest available (Center for the Study of States, 1995).

TWO

WHAT IS A
"FAIR" TAX SYSTEM?

An equitable property tax system is one that treats individuals fairly. Although this definition is simple in concept, difficulties arise when one begins to consider what is meant by *fair*. For example, is the practice of providing property tax relief to elderly homeowners "fair?" Alternatively, how equitable or fair is the practice of assigning different values to different classes of real property for purposes of levying property taxes (e.g., business vs. agricultural property)? The issue of taxpayer equity is complex, and it is difficult to determine with certainty whether a property tax system treats all individuals and businesses fairly. This chapter explores various conceptions of equity. In doing so, our goal is to provide education policy-makers with a framework that enables them to easily identify the important dimensions of taxpayer equity.

Equity Principles

There are two principles of equity that can be employed to determine whether an individual has been treated fairly: *horizontal* and *vertical* equity. Horizontal equity requires the equal treatment of taxpayers in the same, or equal, circumstances. For example, if the property tax is to meet the demands of this principle, all homeowners whose residences have equal values would pay equal amounts of property tax. Or all business property of equal value would pay the same amount of property tax. Notice the identification problems this type of equity principle raises. In particular, reasonable people will sometimes disagree over the value of a given piece of property, and this can interfere with the ability of the system to treat equals equally. As will be discussed in Chapter 4, there are many technical difficulties that surround the determination of property tax levies.

Implicit in the principle of treating equals equally is a willingness to accept the unequal treatment of unequals. This type of inequality contributes to what is called vertical equity. Vertical equity permits the differential treatment of taxpayers in different economic positions. Like horizontal equity, vertical equity raises many complex issues. For example, once allowance is made for the unequal treatment of individual taxpayers, questions must be answered about what it means to be unequal. People who have unequal numbers of children arguably make unequal demands on the educational system for services. Does it follow that school tax liabilities should be similarly unequal? Should only those individuals who use a public service, such as education, be taxed? Alternatively, should individuals be grouped by age, race, sex, income, property wealth, or some combination of these characteristics? To assist in thinking about vertical equity and how taxpayers ought to be classified along various dimensions, two standards have emerged: the *benefit* standard and the *ability to pay* standard.

The Benefit Standard

The benefit standard requires that taxpayers contribute in accordance with the so-called benefits they receive from public services. The more benefits an individual receives, the greater his or her tax burden. There are many examples of the application of the benefit principle in the public sector. For instance, highway and bridge tolls are collected from motorists who use certain thoroughfares, and gasoline taxes are paid on the basis of the number of gallons consumed. Thus, those who drive more, pay more taxes and thereby support to a greater degree the construction and maintenance of highways. Fees collected for the use of buses, subways, trains, and parks also employ the benefit standard, although the distinction between taxes and fees for services is not always clear.

This notion—the more you benefit, the more you pay—aligns nicely with one's sense of fairness. However, when attempts are made to assign the benefits received from a public service to individual taxpayers, the limited applicability of the benefit standard becomes apparent. For example, consider applying the benefit standard to public education. Some may assert that the benefit of public education accrues exclusively to the individual student. Indeed, it is widely acknowledged that higher educational attainment often leads to higher earnings. According to the benefit standard then, the cost of education should be borne only by students or, more reasonably, parents who have children within the public school system.

It is highly probable, however, that nonstudents and those who do not have children in the public school system also derive benefits from an educated populace. For example, society benefits when an education system enables a child to become a scientist, doctor, laborer, or public servant, all of whom may serve a given community. Moreover, higher levels of publicly provided education have been linked to increased economic growth and lower demands for social services such as welfare.

If the benefits of schooling accrue to both individual students and the general public, how can the benefits each taxpayer receives when a child is educated be measured and assigned? Several defensible attempts have been made. It becomes readily apparent, however, that a system that links educational benefits to individuals for purposes of levying taxes is impractical, if not impossible, to define. The application of the benefit standard, therefore, is best reserved for those public services where there is a clear link between the taxpayer, the magnitude of the benefit received, and the associated costs.

The benefit standard also has been rejected on the grounds that it does not afford governments the opportunity to redistribute income. Consider, for example, the provision of social services such as welfare. It would make little sense to tax at higher levels those individuals that benefit most under these programs: the poor.

The Ability Standard

The ability standard is the foundation on which most systems of taxation, including the property tax, rest. Unlike the benefit standard, the ability standard is not concerned with the degree to which individuals benefit from public services. Instead, the ability standard requires that each individual contribute an amount commensurate with his or her fiscal capacity, regardless of the benefits received. In short, those individuals and businesses that are determined to have a greater ability to pay taxes contribute more dollars to the system than those taxpayers who are determined to have a lesser ability to pay.

Two questions need to be answered regarding ability to pay. First, what counts as a measure of ability to pay? In other words, how can we determine a taxpayer's fiscal capacity? And second, depending on a taxpayer's fiscal capacity, what is the appropriate level of contribution? Should taxpayers with twice the ability to pay contribute two, three, or even one and one-half times the amount of tax? The answers to these questions are informed by revisiting the concepts of horizontal and vertical equity.

Horizontal Equity

Recall that horizontal equity is achieved if equals are treated equally. Therefore, it follows that two taxpayers with the same ability to pay should pay the same amount of tax. Although the application of the principle is simple in theory, it is in fact difficult to implement. The difficulty arises from attempts to answer the first question posed earlier: What counts as a measure of ability to pay? If a comprehensive measure of ability to pay could be defined, application of the horizontal equity principle would become routine. However, no such measure exists, and in its place stands a set of indices that measure various aspects of ability to pay. The three most widely employed measures of ability to pay are income, consumption, and wealth.

Income-Based Measures

Income taxes collected at the federal, state, and local levels rely on the income earned by a taxpayer as a measure of his or her ability to pay. Income refers to the inflow of resources within a given time frame. Income includes resources obtained from salaries, wages, dividends, interest, and gains from the sale of assets such as property. An advantage of income as a measure of ability to pay is that it is commonly received in cash or other negotiable instruments, the legal tender in which taxes are paid. A second advantage is that it is time dependent. Time dependence is desirable in that it is possible to match the earnings stream and the payment of taxes. If income varies from year to year, a taxpayer's liability would reflect these differences.

There are, however, drawbacks associated with the use of income as a measure of ability to pay. First, income may take several forms, many of which are difficult to measure. For instance, consider in-kind forms of compensation that accompany jobs in the hospitality or airline industry (e.g., discounts on lodging or tickets). Second, there are forms of income that may be easily hidden or improperly reported. Gratuities earned by service employees serve as the classic example.

Consumption-Based Measures

Underlying the implementation of consumption-based measures is the notion that those who consume more are considered better off than those who consume less. Sales taxes and excise taxes are the most recognizable form of taxes that are based on consumption. The distinction between sales taxes and excise taxes is dependent on the relative selectiveness of the taxing mechanism. General sales taxes apply to broad classes of goods and services (e.g., clothing, appliances, books), whereas excise taxes are applied only to specific items such as alcohol and gasoline.

It is interesting to note that consumption-based measures do not distinguish among sources of revenue. For example, a taxpayer may purchase goods with current or prior income or the sale of assets. Accordingly, consumption-based taxes are based on a more inclusive measure of ability to pay than current income alone.

Wealth-Based Measures

Wealth-based measures seek to determine an individual's wherewithal to pay based on the "value" of resources possessed at a particular point in time. There are several advantages to the use of wealth-based measures as the basis for determining a taxpayer's ability to pay. For example, an individual's wealth might be composed of assets held in the form of cash, stocks, and bonds, all of which are easily valued. Although it is true that taxpayers can hide currency in mattresses and thereby appear to hold fewer assets than is actually the case, these instances are presumably rare. In addition, assets might be held in the form of real property, which is difficult to conceal and can also be assessed and serve as measure of permanent wealth. Historically, wealth as a basis for taxation has looked almost exclusively to real property as a measure of ability to pay.

Despite these advantages, there are disadvantages associated with wealth as a measure of ability to pay. For example, consider the illiquid nature of the real property. An individual taxpayer might hold a sizable amount of real property but receive relatively low levels of income, making it difficult to meet the property tax liability. Recall that property tax obligations must be satisfied with cash or other negotiable instruments. Retired senior citizens who own their homes often find themselves in this situation. In these cases, the wealth-based measure would indicate a relatively high ability to pay. When taxes are levied, elderly homeowners are forced to pay relatively high real property tax bills from low current sources of income. As will be discussed in Chapter 5, the majority of states have implemented tax relief mechanisms that attempt to remedy the illiquid nature of the real property tax.

In addition, the proper specification of what is to be used to determine a taxpayer's wealth (i.e., ability to pay) is paramount if individuals are to be treated fairly. For example, the property tax system, which disallows deductions for liabilities and excludes other personal property, does not accurately reflect the more inclusive financial-based concept of *net worth*. Net worth is defined as assets less liabilities (i.e., debts). To illustrate how the use of the concept of net worth would influence the property tax system, consider the following scenario:

> *All else being equal, two individuals, A and B, both own identical parcels of real property valued at $100,000 each. In addition, A owns the property free and clear, whereas B has a $100,000 mortgage on his respective parcel. Therefore, A has a net worth of $100,000, whereas B has a net worth of $0 ($100,000 asset − $100,000 liability = $0 net worth).*

As the property tax system presently functions, both A's and B's ability to pay will be determined to be equal ($100,000). Accordingly, they will be assessed equal levies. Therefore, in this example, unequals are treated equally. Conversely, if the property tax system measured an individual's net worth, A, whose net worth is higher, would be levied a greater amount commensurate with his holdings. Thus, if one subscribes to the concept of net worth as a more representative measure of an individual's wealth, the property tax system is in violation of principles of equity. In Chapter 4, we explore more fully the operational features of the property tax.

Vertical Equity

The previous discussion dealt with issues concerning the equal treatment of equals, the horizontal equity standard. It is now time to ask the question of what happens when inequality exists in whatever is agreed to be the appropriate measure of ability to pay. For example, how much property tax should taxpayers with twice the value of real property pay? Should they pay two, three, or four times the amount of tax? At issue here is the relationship between the amount of tax and the measure of ability to pay. Because taxes are ultimately paid from income, the relative fairness of a tax instrument is often determined by comparing household tax payments with household personal income.

Depending on how tax payments vary with taxpayer income, tax systems are held to be progressive, proportional, or regressive. In the case of a progressive tax, individuals with higher incomes pay higher proportions of their income in taxes than individuals with lower incomes. For example, an individual with twice the ability to pay would pay greater than two times the amount of tax. With a proportional tax, burdens remain constant across all income groups. Given a proportional tax, twice the ability to pay implies two times the tax; three times the ability to pay implies three times the tax and so on. A proportional tax is often referred to as a *flat tax.*

A regressive tax places a higher tax burden on individuals with lower income than individuals with higher incomes. For example, an individual with twice the ability to pay would pay less than two times the amount of tax, say, one and one-half times the tax obligation. In other words, given a regressive tax instrument, the tax bill of the more able is a smaller percentage of ability to pay than is true for the less able. For example, suppose income is the measure of ability to pay. With a regressive tax, a higher-income person might pay a tax equal to 10% of income, whereas a lower-income person might pay a tax equal to 15%. It is irrelevant that the individual with the higher income pays more tax dollars. The level of progression versus regression in a tax system expresses the relationship between taxes paid and income in percentage terms (often called tax burden), not the

TABLE 2.1 Examples of Progressive, Proportional, and Regressive
Tax Burdens

	Progressive		Proportional		Regressive	
	A	B	A	B	A	B
Income	$25,000	$50,000	$25,000	$50,000	$25,000	$50,000
Taxes paid	$2,500	$7,500	$3,750	$7,500	$3,750	$5,000
Tax burden	10%	15%	15%	15%	15%	10%

NOTE: Tax burden = Taxes paid divided by income

dollars paid. Comparative examples of the three types of tax burdens
are shown in Table 2.1.

Progressive or Regressive?

Considerable debate has emerged in policy circles with regard to
whether taxes should be progressive, proportional, or regressive,
particularly in reference to income taxes. Arguments have been
made in favor of and in opposition to progression in the tax rate
structures. Advocates for greater equality in economic life assert that
progression implies the need for a redistribution of resources from
the more able to the less able to pay. Moreover, progression has been
justified based on an idea called *sacrifice theory*. Sacrifice theory presumes that an extra dollar earned is worth less to a wealthy person
than a poor person.

Opponents of progression argue that progressive rate structures
excessively complicate the tax system and reduce incentives to earn.
Opponents also suggest that progressive rate structures may lead to
political irresponsibility by allowing the more numerous lower-
income taxpayers to join together and impose higher tax rates on the
relatively small number of higher-income taxpayers.[1]

It is important to recognize that although policymakers can debate the relative merits of progression in tax systems, they cannot
disregard the social setting in which these fiscal policies operate. It is
generally perceived by the public that a regressive tax is an undesirable tax that offends conceptions of equity as it relates to measures
of ability to pay. Recent education finance reform efforts stemming

from the alleged regressivity of the property tax serve as testament to the importance of acknowledging the public's perceptions of fairness in structuring finance systems. More will be said of the perceived regressiveness of the property tax in the following chapter.

Problems in Measuring Tax Progression

It is one thing to say that progression is favorable to regression but another thing to agree on how much progression should be built into a tax system. For example, it may be agreed on that some degree of income redistribution is necessary if impoverished parents are to improve the life chances of their children. However, it does not follow that perfect equality in the distribution of resources is required to meet this objective.

If perfect equality is not the goal, how much progression or how little regression is desirable? The difficulty of this question is complicated by the fact that the precise magnitude of progression or regression in a tax system is often difficult to determine. Part of the problem results from the distinction that must be drawn between the perceived and actual degree of progression associated with a particular tax. For example, the present federal income tax includes marginal tax rates that range from 15% to 39.6% for single taxpayers. This rate structure suggests there is an element of progression in the tax system. Keep in mind, however, that numerous exceptions are made on what counts as taxable income. For example, certain types of income receive preferential tax treatment, such as tax-exempt interest on specified municipal bonds. In addition, deductions are permitted for medical expenses, business expenses, local taxes, and charitable contributions, to name only a few. To the degree that these deductions and exemptions apply more to the wealthy than the poor, the actual magnitude of progression in the tax system is reduced. On the other hand, if poor taxpayers are granted exemptions from certain portions of their tax bill, the regressiveness of the tax is reduced. Therefore, there can be a high degree of perceived or nominal progressiveness (regressiveness) in a given tax instrument with an actual impact that is proportionate or even regressive (progressive).

Additional problems in measuring tax progression become apparent when one recognizes that the statutory taxpayer, the one who actually pays the tax collector, sometimes differs from the taxpayer(s) on which the tax burden actually falls. Assessing the incidence of a tax recognizes that taxes can be shifted among different classes of taxpayers. For example, consider what group most likely bears the burden of property taxes on rental property. The property taxes are paid by landlords. Landlords, however, may pass some portion of the cost of property taxes on to renters in the form of higher rents. If the tax is borne by low-income renters, the property tax will be more regressive than initially appears to be the case. Similarly, depending on the particular industry, property taxes on businesses can be passed on to consumers in the form of higher prices, to employees in the form of lower salaries and wages, or to shareholders in the form of reduced dividends. The actual incidence or coming to rest of the tax must be known before it becomes possible to measure the relative degree of progression or regression in a tax system. It turns out that assumptions about the degree of shifting that occurs among taxpayers has produced disparate conclusions on the regressivity or progressivity of taxes such as the property tax. In Chapter 3, we reexamine the debate over who bears the burden of the real property tax.

Last, there are measurement problems because taxpayers face a variety of tax instruments. Should the relative progressiveness that a taxpayer faces be measured in reference to a single type of tax, say income, or should progression be measured in light of all taxes? The incidence of one instrument may be progressive, whereas another may be regressive. Similarly, taxpayers pay different amounts of taxes depending on where they live. Consider differences in property and sales tax rates that often exist between neighboring jurisdictions.

Final Comments

Taxes are expected to be equitable. In short, an equitable tax system is one that treats individuals fairly. As the foregoing discussion makes clear, there are many ways to conceptualize and define what is meant by "fair." What is most important for readers to take from this discussion is that the relative fairness of a tax system should be assessed in reference to individual tax burdens, not total dollars paid. Indeed, it is possible that individuals with higher property tax bills actually have lower tax burdens relative to poorer homeowners.

Policymakers interested in changing the existing structure of school finance need to be attentive to who ultimately bears the burdens of school taxes.

Note

1. This discussion only highlights the debate concerning progression in tax systems. Readers interested in more detailed descriptions of the pros and cons of progression are encouraged to turn to Walter J. Blum and Harry Klaven Jr.'s classic discourse on tax progression (Blum & Klaven, 1953).

THREE

HOW SHOULD EDUCATION'S
TAXES BE EVALUATED?

The equity concepts discussed in Chapter 2 provide a useful starting point for considering the merits or shortcomings of a given tax instrument. The notion of fairness, however, is not the only issue that needs to be addressed when assessing the desirability of the property tax for purposes of funding public education. Indeed, although a dollar earned through the property tax will support the same level of public services as a dollar earned through either the sales tax or income tax, each tax instrument influences different economic, political, and social forces (Gold, 1994). For example, some taxes are more stable sources of revenue, whereas others demonstrate greater growth potential. Policymakers interested in altering the current mix of public support for education need to consider these differences. In this chapter, we evaluate the desirability of using income, sales, and property taxes for the purpose of funding education. Detailed discussions of specific education finance reform proposals are reserved for later chapters. The intent here is to provide a framework for evaluating the desirability of proposed changes to existing structures of local school finance.

Public finance theory suggests that there are least seven attributes that need to be considered when evaluating a given tax: equity or fairness, efficiency, potential for economic growth, stability, administration, compliance, and public acceptance.[1]

Equity or Fairness

First, we turn our attention to the relative fairness of the three primary education taxes: personal income tax, sales tax, and property tax. To the degree that these taxes display elements of progressivity, they will be deemed favorable. If, however, the taxes are found to be regressive, the use of these taxes to support public education is suspect.

Personal Income Tax

Many states impose a tax on personal income. Table 3.1 presents state individual income tax rates for tax year 1996.

At first glance, most state personal income tax systems appear to be progressive. For example, Ohio has a graduated income tax with rates ranging between 0.693% and 7.004% of taxable income. Rhode Island's income tax rate is defined as 27.5% of federal income tax liability. New Hampshire and Tennessee's state income tax is limited to dividends and interest income only, both sources of income that are more likely to be earned by wealthier taxpayers.

Although the existence of graduated brackets points directly toward a state's desire to create a progressive rate structure (i.e., the tax rates increase as income rises), several underlying features of the system can significantly reduce the progressivity of the income tax. For example, the highest tax rate in Wisconsin starts at a relatively low level of taxable income, $15,000. Although having the highest tax rate take effect at a low-income level increases tax revenue, it also reduces the progressivity of the tax (Gold, 1994).

Compression or narrowing of the tax brackets also reduces the progressivity of state income tax systems (Gold, 1994). In New York, for example, the Tax Reform and Reduction Act of 1987 provides for a compression of the income tax brackets. In 1986, the bottom tax rate was 2%, whereas the highest tax rate was 9.5% for earned income and 13.5% for unearned income. As indicated, the current rates are 4% and 7% for both earned and unearned income. In 1997, the year when the provisions of the Act are to be fully implemented, the bottom bracket will rise to 5.5%, whereas the highest bracket for earned and unearned income will decrease to 7.0%. Compression of the tax

TABLE 3.1 State Individual Income Tax Rates, Tax Year 1997

State	Number of Brackets	Tax Rates		Income Brackets ($)	
		Low	High	Lows	High
Alabama	3	2.00	5.00	500	3,000
Alaska	No state income tax				
Arizona	5	3.00	5.60	10,000	150,000
Arkansas	6	1.00	7.00	2,999	25,000
California	6	1.00	9.30	4,908	223,390
Colorado	1	5.00		Flat rate	
Connecticut	2	3.00	4.50	2,250	2,250
Delaware	7	0.00	6.90	4,500	30,000
District of Columbia	3	6.00	9.50	10,000	20,000
Florida	No state income tax				
Georgia	6	1.00	6.00	750	7,000
Hawaii	8	2.00	10.00	1,500	20,500
Idaho	8	2.00	8.20	1,000	20,000
Illinois	1	3.00		Flat rate	
Indiana	1	3.40		Flat rate	
Iowa	9	0.40	9.98	1,081	48,645
Kansas	3	4.40	7.75	20,000	30,000
Kentucky	5	2.00	6.00	3,000	8,000
Louisiana	3	2.00	6.00	10,000	50,000
Maine	4	2.00	8.50	4,150	16,500
Maryland	4	2.00	5.00	1,000	3,000
Massachusetts	1	5.95		Flat rate	
Michigan	1	4.40		Flat rate	
Minnesota	3	6.00	8.50	16,510	54,250
Mississippi	3	3.00	5.00	5,000	10,000
Missouri	10	1.50	6.00	1,000	9,000
Montana	10	2.00	11.00	1,900	66,399
Nebraska	4	2.62	6.99	2,400	26,500
Nevada	No state income tax				
New Hampshire	State income tax is limited to dividends and interest income only				
New Jersey	6	1.40	6.37	20,000	75,000
New Mexico	7	1.70	8.50	5,500	65,000

TABLE 3.1 continued

State	Number of Brackets	Tax Rates Low	High	Income Brackets ($) Lows	High
New York	4	4.00	7.00	5,500	11,000
North Carolina	3	6.00	7.75	12,750	60,000
North Dakota	8	2.67	12.00	3,000	50,000
Ohio	9	0.693	7.004	5,000	200,000
Oklahoma	8	0.50	7.00	1,000	10,000
Oregon	3	5.00	9.00	2,150	5,400
Pennsylvania	1	2.80		Flat Rate	
Rhode Island	27.5% federal tax liability				
South Carolina	6	2.50	7.00	2,280	11,400
South Dakota	No state income tax				
Tennessee	State income tax is limited to dividends and interest income only				
Texas	No state income tax				
Utah	6	2.3	7.00	750	3,750
Vermont	25% federal tax liability				
Virginia	4	2.00	5.75	3,000	17,000
Washington	No state income tax				
West Virginia	5	3.00	6.50	10,000	60,000
Wisconsin	3	4.90	6.93	7,500	15,000
Wyoming	No state income tax				

SOURCE: Federation of Tax Administrators
(http://sso.org/fta/ind_inc.html).

brackets will make New York's personal income tax look more like a proportional tax than a progressive tax.

Despite the potentiality of low rate ceilings and compression of the tax brackets to influence the progressivity of the tax system, evidence suggests that, in general, state income taxes remain progressive. It is interesting to note, however, that seven states (Alaska, Florida, Nevada, South Dakota, Texas, Washington, and Wyoming) have no state income tax, and six states (Colorado, Illinois, Indiana, Massachusetts, Michigan, and Pennsylvania) impose a proportional income tax rate.

Sales Tax

The general sales tax is widely held to be a regressive tax (e.g., Pechman, 1986). In other words, low-income taxpayers devote a greater proportion of their incomes to paying sales taxes relative to high-income taxpayers. For example, high-income individuals are more likely to spend more of their income on housing (owners and renters), investments, and savings, all of which are not subject to sales taxation. In contrast, low-income individuals are more likely to spend larger percentages of their income on food, clothing, and other necessities, many of which are subject to sales taxation (Odden & Picus, 1992). Thus, although high-income and low-income taxpayers pay the same rate of sales tax, poorer taxpayers bear a greater burden.

Caution should be exercised before judgment is passed on to the magnitude of regressivity of the sales tax. Indeed, the degree of regressivity depends on what is included in the sales tax base. In many states, for example, most food items and both prescription and nonprescription medicine are exempt. These exclusions tend to make the sales tax less regressive. Often, however, states also exempt professional services, such as legal, medical, accounting, and architecture. To the extent that these services are provided to higher-income households, the sales tax becomes more regressive (Gold, 1994). Therefore, although it is widely accepted that the sales tax is regressive, the degree of regressivity remains unclear.

Property Tax

Due to difficulties in determining who actually bears the burden of the property tax (i.e., incidence), there is considerable debate as to whether property tax burdens in total (i.e., all classes of property) are regressive or progressive (e.g., Pechman, 1985; Wildasin, 1987). Despite these difficulties, it is widely accepted that the tax on low-income renters and residential property owners is regressive. Regressivity occurs for low-income renters because these individuals devote a large proportion of their income to rental payments, and low-income homeowners (many of whom are elderly) devote a large proportion of their income to the payment of property taxes (Gold, 1994).

To help compensate for the regressivity that occurs at low-income levels, the majority of states have implemented mechanisms to provide property tax relief to poor and elderly homeowners. The relief, termed *circuit breakers* and *homestead exemptions*, generally come in the form of income tax credits for a portion of property taxes paid or a direct reduction of the property tax bill. Property tax relief mechanisms are explored in detail in Chapter 5.

Efficiency

Most taxes not only lighten one's pocket but influence where and what consumers purchase, the homes people buy, and the location decisions of businesses. When a tax distorts decisions such as these, it results in what economists call *excess burden*. Excess burden represents a loss in welfare, often called *utility*, above and beyond the tax revenues collected (Rosen, 1992). Consider the following example:

> *The Smith family has saved $10,000 for the purpose of building a new garage on their home. The local school district levies a property tax so that the Smiths will face a higher tax bill if they build a garage because of the resulting increase in the value of their residence. In response to the potential increase in property taxes, the Smiths decide not to build the garage and instead, spend the money on other goods and services. Because the Smiths spent no money on the garage, they pay no additional property tax. But can we say that the Smith's are unaffected by the tax? The answer is no. The Smiths are worse off because the tax induced them not to build the garage. We know that the purchase of other goods and services was less desirable because the Smiths had had the option of doing so but chose instead to save for the garage. Thus, even though the Smiths did not have to pay additional property taxes, the tax altered their behavior.*

The excess burdens caused by taxes are directly related to the tax rate (Gold, 1994). In general, the higher the tax rate, the greater the possibility for the tax to distort a taxpayer's behavior. To the extent that a tax distorts decision making, the effects interfere with the efficient operation of the economy.[2]

Income Tax

New York has the highest nominal personal income tax rate in the mid-Atlantic states: 7.0% (see Table 3.1). New York State Tax Law also authorizes the city of New York and the city of Yonkers to impose personal income taxes on their residents. If these income tax add-ons and the state's high tax rate encourage individuals to move from New York to other states or discourage investing and saving, the taxes will have influenced economic behavior and are therefore inefficient. Other states with high nominal personal income tax rates are California, Hawaii, Montana, North Dakota, and Oregon. In contrast, recall that seven states have no state income tax (Alaska, Florida, Nevada, South Dakota, Texas, Washington, and Wyoming).

One must be careful, however, not to view the rate of income tax without regard for potentially mitigating factors. For example, the deductibility of state income taxes on federal returns reduces the incentive to move in response to state income taxes (i.e., it lowers the effective state income tax rate). More important, taxpayers may feel that the increased rate supports more or better public services.

Sales Tax

In general, state sales taxes apply to nearly all retail sales of tangible personal property and to certain services. Many states' sales tax laws also allow for local sales taxes, administered at the county or municipal level (see Table 3.2). For example, Pennsylvania not only imposes a sales tax at the state level but permits the cities of Philadelphia and Pittsburgh and Allegheny County to levy additional sales taxes.

When a state or locality's sales tax is much higher than its neighbors', the tax is likely to influence the behavior of purchasers. For example, unlike Pennsylvania and New Jersey, New York State does not exempt clothing purchases from the sales tax. Therefore, New Yorkers who live near the state borders are provided with an incentive to make clothing purchases in either Pennsylvania or New Jersey. Differences in local sales tax rates across counties and municipalities can result in similar influences on spending behaviors within a state.

Property Tax

It is widely known that property tax burdens can vary widely among local districts within a given state. In fact, property tax burdens are often found to vary significantly among neighboring districts in the same county. For example, in one New York county,

TABLE 3.2 State-Local General Sales Taxes: Combined Rates, Selected Cities, 1993

State	City (County)	State Sales Tax	County Sales Tax	City Sales Tax	Other Sales Tax	Total Sales Tax
Alabama	Birmingham	4.00	1.00	3.00		8.00
	Mobile	4.00	1.00	4.00		9.00
Alaska	Juneau			4.00		4.00
Arizona	Phoenix	5.00	0.50	1.30		6.70
	Tucson	5.00		2.00		7.00
Arkansas	Little Rock	4.50	1.00	5.50		
California	Los Angeles	6.00	1.25		1.00	8.25
	San Diego	6.00	1.25		0.50	7.75
	San Francisco	6.00	1.25		1.25	8.50
Colorado	Boulder	3.00		2.86	0.80	6.66
	Denver	3.00		3.50	0.80	7.30
Connecticut		6.00	No local sales tax			6.00
Delaware		No state or local sales tax				
District of Columbia		6.00				6.00
Florida	Jacksonville	6.00	0.50			6.50
	Miami	6.00	0.50			6.50
Georgia	Atlanta	4.00	1.00		1.00	6.00
	Savannah	4.00	1.00			5.00
Hawaii		4.00	No local sales tax			4.00
Idaho	Boise	5.00				5.00
	Sun Valley	5.00		2.00		7.00
Illinois	Chicago	6.25	0.75	1.00	0.75	8.75
	Rockford	6.25				6.25
Indiana		5.00	No local sales tax			5.00
Iowa	Des Moines	5.00				5.00
	Dubuque	5.00		1.00		6.00
Kansas	Kansas City	4.90	1.00	1.00		6.90
	Wichita	4.90	1.00			5.90
Kentucky		6.00	No local sales tax			6.00

(continued)

TABLE 3.2 continued

State	City (County)	State Sales Tax	County Sales Tax	City Sales Tax	Other Sales Tax	Total Sales Tax
Louisiana	Baton Rouge	4.00	2.00	2.00		8.00
	New Orleans	4.00	5.00			9.00
	Shreveport	4.00	3.00	2.50		9.50
Maine		6.00	No local sales tax			6.00
Maryland		5.00	No local sales tax			5.00
Massachusetts		5.00	No local sales tax			5.00
Michigan		4.00	No local sales tax			4.00
Minnesota	Minneapolis	6.00	0.50	0.50		7.00
	St. Paul	6.00	0.50			6.50
Mississippi		7.00	No local sales tax			7.00
Missouri	Kansas City	4.225	1.00	0.75	0.50	6.475
	St. Louis	4.225		1.00	0.50	5.725
Montana		No state or local sales tax				
Nebraska	Lincoln	5.00		1.50		6.50
Nevada	Las Vegas	6.50	0.50			7.00
New Hampshire		No state or local sales tax				
New Jersey		6.00	No local sales tax			6.00
New Mexico	Albuquerque	5.00	0.375	0.4375		5.8125
	Santa Fe	5.00	0.75	0.375		6.125
New York	Albany	4.00	4.00			8.00
	New York City	4.00		4.25		8.25
	Syracuse	4.00	3.00			7.00
North Carolina	Charlotte	4.00	2.00			6.00
	Raleigh	4.00	2.00			6.00
North Dakota	Fargo	5.00		1.00		6.00
Ohio	Cincinnati	5.00	0.50			5.50
	Cleveland	5.00	2.00			7.00
Oklahoma	Oklahoma City	4.50		2.875		7.375
	Tulsa	4.50		3.00		7.50

State	City (County)	State Sales Tax	County Sales Tax	City Sales Tax	Other Sales Tax	Total Sales Tax
Oregon						
Pennsylvania	Philadelphia	6.00		1.00		7.00
	Pittsburgh	6.00		1.00		7.00
Rhode Island		7.00	No local sales tax			7.00
South Carolina	Charleston	5.00	1.00			6.00
South Dakota	Rapid City	4.00		2.00		6.00
Tennessee	Nashville	6.00	2.25			8.25
Texas	Austin	6.25		1.00	0.75	8.00
	Dallas	6.25		1.00	1.00	8.25
	Houston	6.25		1.00	1.00	8.25
Utah	Salt Lake City	5.00	1.00		0.25	6.25
Vermont		5.00	No local sales tax			5.00
Virginia	Alexandria	3.50		1.00		4.50
	Richmond	3.50		1.00		4.50
Washington	Seattle	6.50		1.70		8.20
	Spokane	6.50		1.30		7.80
West Virginia		6.00	No local sales tax			6.00
Wisconsin	Milwaukee	5.00	0.50			5.50
Wyoming	Lincoln	3.00	1.00			4.00

SOURCE: Adapted from Advisory Commission on Intergovernmental Relations (ACIR; 1994), *Significant Features of Fiscal Federalism: Vol. 1,* Table 32.

effective property tax rates have ranged from 4.16% to 21.75% per $1,000 full value.

To the extent that individuals and businesses make location decisions based on tax burdens alone, the property tax will be deemed to be inefficient. Caution needs to be exercised, however, not to label the property tax inefficient solely because property tax rates vary among districts. Indeed, several studies suggest that disparities in state and local property tax rates are simply too small to offset differences in more basic determinants of business location, such as labor costs and accessibility to markets (Ladd & Bradbury, 1988). Lower property tax rates may also result in higher purchase prices for property. In addition, movement between districts might not be motivated by tax burdens alone but rather by the entire fiscal package. That is, potential residents may be willing to pay higher taxes in one jurisdiction than another if higher taxes are offset by higher services. For example, the Smiths might determine that the amount and quality of public education in a given community is greater and therefore they are willing to incur a greater property tax burden.

It is quite easy to find published reports on the tax rates faced by individuals and businesses. You would look in vain, however, to find any mention in these documents of the excess burden caused by any of the three primary education taxes. The reason is easy to understand. Excess burden is a rather conceptually straightforward notion that is difficult to measure. Nevertheless, although losses of welfare that accompanying tax-induced changes in behavior are often hidden, they are real and should be considered when assessing the merits of a given tax system (Rosen, 1992).

Potential for Economic Growth

One of the primary purposes of taxation is to raise revenues for public services. Because the cost of providing public services is likely to change over time, taxes should be responsive to shifts in the economy. For example, education costs are likely to rise due to inflation, increased enrollments, and the additional costs associated with at-risk students. It is desirable for education tax revenues to grow as well.

The relative degree to which a tax responds to changes in the economy is stated in terms of the tax's *elasticity*. Elasticity is measured by calculating the percentage increase in tax base (i.e., tax dollars collected) that results from a 1% increase in personal income. A tax that raises revenue proportionately with increases in income has an elasticity of 1.0; taxes that raise revenues faster than increases in income are referred to as elastic (i.e., elasticity greater than 1.0); and taxes that raise revenues slower than increases in income are said to be inelastic (i.e., elasticity less than 1.0).

Income Taxes

The income tax is the only major tax instrument that has an elasticity greater than 1.0 (Mikesell, 1986). In other words, as incomes rise, more income tax revenues are generated. The elasticity of the income tax is largely the result of the progressive structure of the tax. For instance, as income rises throughout the economy, more individuals are moved into higher tax brackets, generating more tax revenue for the state. Accordingly, states and localities can make the income tax more or less elastic by making the system more or less progressive.

Although income taxes are generally responsive to economic growth, many states have taken steps to reduce the elasticity of its personal income tax. Recall that New York State compressed its income tax rate structure, thereby decreasing the progressivity of the system. The flattening of the tax rate brackets makes personal income taxes less responsive to changes in the economy.

Sales Tax

The elasticity of the general sales tax is believed to be approximately 1.0 (Mikesell, 1986). In other words, as incomes rise, so too does the revenue generated by the sales tax. The elasticity of the sales tax is largely dependent on the composition of its base. For example, the demand for food is not very responsive to changes in the economy. If food is taxed, the elasticity of the sales tax tends to be lower. In contrast, the demand for professional services is closely linked to shifts in the economy (Dye & Mcquire, 1992). If professional services, such as accounting and architecture fees, are taxed, the sales tax can be highly elastic.

Property Tax

A major criticism of the property tax is that the tax base is not responsive to economic growth. Indeed, its elasticity has been estimated to be well below 1.0 (Mikesell, 1986). In other words, as incomes rise, the revenue generated from the property tax increases much more slowly. As a consequence, government units that are largely dependent on property taxes as a source of revenue (e.g., schools) must continually raise their rates to accommodate increases in the demand for public service such as education. This phenomenon may be particularly troubling in states where a large percentage of school district revenues are secured from the property tax.

Stability of Revenues

All else being equal, a tax that produces consistent amounts of revenue each year is preferable to a tax whose revenue stream is unpredictable. If revenue streams are unstable, state and local governments will have great difficulty ensuring that sufficient resources are available to meet their fiscal needs. On the other hand, a tax that is stable and produces a predictable flow of tax dollars does not respond well to changes in the economy. Unfortunately, there is a trade-off between a tax instrument's potential for economic growth (i.e., elasticity) and its stability.

Income Tax

Although increasing reliance on the income tax might make education taxes more responsive to shifts in the economy, it also decreases the stability of the revenue source. In the 1990s, this phenomenon has proven to be troublesome to school systems in many states. For example, in the 1980s, California's primary source of school district revenue shifted from the local level (i.e., property taxes) to the state level (i.e., income and sales taxes). In the 1990s, a slowed-down state economy caused the state to experience significant budget shortfalls. As a result, spending on kindergarten through 12th grade (K-12) education has remained relatively flat in California throughout the decade. The state has been able to fund growth in the number of students but has been unable to compensate districts for increased costs due to inflation.

Sales Tax

If the sales tax is levied on goods or services for which demand does not fluctuate (i.e., inelastic), the tax will be relatively stable. For example, the taxation of food contributes to the stability of the state's sales tax system. In contrast, if states exempt goods such as food from the sales tax base, as is the case in the majority of states, the stability of the tax as a source of revenue falls.

Property Tax

One of the primary benefits of using the property tax to fund public schools is its stability relative to other taxes. Recall that the elasticity of the property tax was less than 1.0, indicating that in both good times and bad times, the tax produces a relatively constant stream of revenue. This presumes, of course, that in downturns in the economy, local governments will be able to collect the property tax, a problem that has proven to be particularly troublesome in many states. For example, during the last decade, arrearages or missed payments of school property taxes have increased dramatically in several states (e.g., 40% in New York). Although county or state governments are often required to foot the bill for delinquent taxpayers, continued forfeitures bring into question the stability of the tax.

Administration and Compliance

All broad-based taxes, such as income, sales, and property taxes, require administrative costs for both the government and the individuals on which they are levied. In general, tax administration and compliance involve seven steps (Mikesell, 1986): (a) maintaining and gathering records, (b) computing the tax liability, (c) remittance of tax liability, (d) collection, (e) audit, (f) appeal, and (g) enforcement. Depending on what type of tax instrument is employed, the responsibility for performing these steps falls on either individual taxpayers or government agencies. Ideally, both the administration of the tax and the individual's ability to comply with the requirements of the tax should be as low cost and simple as possible. As a rule of thumb, the more complicated the tax system, the greater the costs of both administration and compliance.

Income Taxes

Income tax systems require the taxpayer, individuals or businesses, to perform the first three steps outlined in the previous paragraph. For example, to satisfy their liability, taxpayers are required to gather accounting records, compute the tax liability, and then file a return. Because taxpayers are required to perform these steps, state income taxes are complex and costly for many individuals and businesses (Mikesell, 1986). Studies have estimated that taxpayers spend approximately 29 hours preparing their individual state and federal income tax returns annually. Moreover, taxpayers unable to prepare their personal returns must employ accountants, lawyers, and other tax services to assist in compliance. Those who have sought professional advice are well aware of the costs in time and money incurred during the preparation of their income returns. States that closely align state reporting requirements with federal guidelines likely reduce the costs of administration of the state income tax.

The costs associated with steps (d) through (g) are largely borne by state or local governments. The costs of the fourth step, collection, fall exclusively on the government unit. The government is not only responsible for the costs of administering the filing of income tax returns but also for providing information that facilitates the preparation of these returns. For example, states provide taxpayers with income tax forms and offices that assist taxpayers in filing these forms. The fifth step, audit, serves a twofold purpose for the state or local government. First, it seeks to encourage voluntary compliance with the tax laws by discovering omissions and misstatements by dishonest taxpayers. Second, it seeks to remedy honest taxpayer misinterpretations of complex tax laws (Mikesell, 1986). If an error is found in an income tax return, the taxpayer is given the option of appealing the government's finding, the seventh step. Appeals help clarify the difficult-to-understand areas that surround many provisions of state income tax codes. Last, enforcement results when the taxpayer has failed to submit the required income tax liability.

Studies of state income tax systems estimate that administrative costs as a percentage of net revenue range from 0.64% to 0.81% (e.g., Mikesell, 1986). What is encouraging from an administrative perspective is that most revenue comes from voluntary compliance. In other words, little revenue is raised from the audit or enforcement actions. For example, Table 3.3 presents a recent summary of New Jersey's income tax collections.

Tax avoidance, paying the minimum level of tax required by the law, is legal. Tax evasion, cheating, is not. Table 3.3 tells us little about the amount of income tax revenue that is lost when people intentionally shortchange the government. There are several ways to commit tax evasion (Rosen, 1992):

1. Keep two sets of accounting records. The first set of books records the actual transactions conducted by a business. The

TABLE 3.3 New Jersey State Income Tax Collections by Source

Source	Percent of Collections
Billings for penalties and interest	0.30
Delinquency phone calls, letters	0.05
Delinquency investigations	0.33
Bankruptcies, liens, etc.	0.68
Office audits	0.52
Field audits	0.89
Voluntary compliance	97.23
Total	100.00

SOURCE: Adapted from Mikesell (1986).

second, which underreports income or overreports expenses, is used for purposes of preparing tax returns.

2. Underreport tips and wages. Tips paid to waiters, waitresses, beauticians, valets, and so forth, are taxable income. These types of earnings are difficult to trace and are notoriously underreported. Wages paid in cash, commonly termed *under-the-table*, also often go unreported to taxing authorities.

3. Make in-kind payments. "If you fix my car, I'll paint your house" is another example of a transaction that results in income earned but is unlikely to be reported.

The amount of income tax evasion that occurs in a given state is difficult to measure. On the federal level, it is estimated that approximately $85 billion of income goes unreported each year (Rosen, 1992). If this estimate is accurate, it suggests that income tax evasion is a serious issue that adds to the cost of administering such a tax.

Sales Tax

Commercial entities who sell goods or services subject to the sales tax are required to register with the state and follow the procedures for collecting and remitting the tax receipts to the designated authority (e.g., state, county, city). In this case, it is the merchant, not the taxpayer, that bears the costs of compliance.

At both the state and local levels, the administration of the sales tax is neither complex nor costly. Indeed, state sales tax law is less complicated than many of the other taxes that states administer. Estimates of the costs to administer the tax as a percentage of net revenue is only 0.37 (Mikesell, 1986). This figure is significantly lower than the costs to administer the income tax, as specified earlier.

Property Tax

A generalized view of the administration of the property tax follows: First, the district establishes a tax rate, which is then applied to the assessed value of each individual's property to determine the respective tax bill; municipal officials then collect the school taxes, along with all other property taxes for the governmental unit; last, the school tax revenues are then distributed back to the district from which they were generated. In the administration of the property tax, the taxpayer assumes a passive role. That is, valuation and collection has been reserved by the local taxing authority. From the taxpayer's perspective, unless the taxpayer appeals an assessment, costs of compliance require only that they remit payment to the local authority. In contrast, the cost to the government of administering a so-called good-quality property tax system has been estimated at 1.5% of collections, significantly more than the costs estimated for either income or sales taxes (Mikesell, 1986). Much more will be said about property assessment practices in upcoming chapters.

Public Acceptance

Is a tax fair? Is a tax efficient? Is a tax easy to comply with? All of these questions may have a bearing on whether a tax instrument is accepted by the public. As Table 3.4 reveals, several interesting observations can be made regarding the public's perceptions of various tax mechanisms. First, local property tax consistently is regarded as the worst tax. Not only is the property tax deemed to be the worst overall tax, but as evidenced by the table, it is perceived to be much less desirable than the other two primary education taxes, income and sales taxes. It is interesting that when only state income taxes and state sales taxes are compared, income taxes are viewed more favorably. Other studies (Gold, 1994) have also reported the following:

TABLE 3.4 Public Perceptions of Taxes

Which Tax Do You Think Is the Worst Tax—That Is, the Least Fair?

Year	Federal Income Tax	Social Security Tax	State Income Tax	State Sales Tax	Local Property Tax	Don't Know
1994	27%	12%	7%	14%	28%	11%
1993			Question not asked			
1992	25	10	9	16	25	15
1991			Question not asked			
1990	26	15	10	12	28	9
1989	21	18	9	14	28	10
1988	26	17	9	15	24	9

SOURCE: Adapted from Advisory Commission on Intergovernmental Relations (1994), *Changing Public Attitudes on Governments and Taxes,* Table 2.

- Increasing sales taxes are preferred over across-the-board income tax increases.
- Increasing taxes on the wealthy and businesses is popular, as is loophole closing.
- Increasing existing taxes are preferred over enactment of new taxes.

It is not surprising that individuals tend to prefer taxes they perceive will be paid by someone else, such as the wealthy and businesses. Public approval of increasing business taxes, however, ignores the fact that, at least in some cases, the burden will be passed on to consumers in the form of higher prices and to workers through lower wages. The public also appears to prefer taxes that are paid in relatively small amounts on a daily, weekly, or biweekly basis (i.e., income and sales). In contrast, the property tax requires larger, less frequent payments (Gold, 1994).

Final Comments

Although each of the three major taxes used to support public education has strengths, all have weaknesses as well. Some taxes are more equitable. The mildly progressive nature of the personal income tax in the majority of states suggests that this tax is the most fair of the education taxes. The high-income tax rates in several states also contribute to the ability of the income tax's to respond to growth in the economy. Unlike the property tax, however, the state income tax is unstable. Thus, whereas a dollar earned from the property tax equals a dollar earned from the income tax, policymakers interested in altering the education tax mix must address economic as well as political concerns.

Two general observations can be made from the foregoing analysis. First, the higher a tax's rate, the greater its "imperfections" (Gold, 1994). This would suggest that it is desirable to have a relatively well-balanced tax system that makes use of income, sales, and property taxes to support education. This holds particularly true in states where the state-local tax burden for all taxes is well above the national average. Second, because education is financed through a variety of taxes, policymakers need to look at how the whole tax package measures up against the seven attributes employed to evaluate tax systems. For example, the regressive natures of the property tax and sales tax can be mitigated by the progressive nature of the income tax. Similarly, the responsiveness and instability of income and sales taxes can be offset by the inelastic but stable property tax.

It does not appear that states' most pressing concern should be what tax to abandon for purposes of financing education. Rather, how can they fine tune the taxes already employed? Because the property tax accounts for approximately 47% of the total revenues raised for education, it should be first on the list for reform. Improvements in administrative practices alone can do much to enhance both the equity (e.g., circuit breakers) and political acceptability of the tax. It may be the case after such reforms are in place that the perceived need to make abrupt changes in the education tax mix will subside.

Notes

1. This discussion draws on the framework for comparing taxes developed by Gold (1994).

2. See Rosen (1992) for a comprehensive discussion of taxes and efficiency.

FOUR

HOW DOES THE
PROPERTY TAX WORK?

It is important for anyone interested in how revenues are raised for schools to have a good grasp of how the property tax works. In theory, the operation of the property tax is quite simple. In practice, however, the operation of the property tax is anything but simple. In fact, each state and many localities within individual states are governed by their own sets of rules that prescribe how property taxes will be levied. It is not our intent to uncover all of the nuances that differentiate property tax administration among jurisdictions. Instead, the purpose of this chapter is to explain the operation of the property tax with an emphasis on what contributes to the complexity in practice. The strengths and weaknesses of individual property tax administrative practices are explored in upcoming chapters.

Identifying the Property Tax Base

The property tax is a tax on wealth, or more accurately, wealth that takes the form of property. The first question that needs to be answered is what will count as property for purposes of taxation? The answer to this question is known as the *property tax base.*

Property can take numerous forms, and states vary in how they treat different types of property for tax purposes. In general, property can be classified in any one of three broad groups: *real property, tangible personal property,* and *intangible personal property.* Real property refers to land and any permanently attached improvements, such as commercial buildings and residential houses. Tangible personal property is comprised of assets other than real property that have physical substance. Tangible personal property includes such property as business equipment, inventory, automobiles, and computers. In contrast, intangible personal property includes assets that do not have physical substance that are held by taxpayers because of the use of the rights or exchange value they confer to the owner. Examples of intangible personal property are cash, stocks, bonds, copyrights, patents, and trademarks.

As Table 4.1 reveals, states differ in the types of property that are included in the property tax base. Six states (Delaware, Hawaii, Illinois, New Hampshire, New York, South Dakota) exempt all tangible and intangible property from property taxation. Thirty states exempt all intangible personal property. On the other hand, all states subject real property to property taxation. In fact, locally assessed real property accounts for approximately 87% of the total net assessed value for all property (Census of Governments, 1992). See Table 4.2 for these comparisons.

Perhaps one reason real property is always used in determining the tax base for property tax purposes is that it is an immobile asset that is difficult to conceal. This is less true for personal property. For instance, it is much easier to conceal a piece of jewelry, an automobile, or a television set than it is to hide a parcel of land or a building. It is even more difficult, particularly at the local level, to monitor holdings of intangible property, such as stocks, bonds, and cash. Rather than attempt to levy a tax on these highly mobile and easily concealed types of property, these assets are more often taxed on their sale or transfer.

Assigning Value to the Tax Base

Before property can be taxed, it must be valued. Assigning value to property is the responsibility of a local official called the *assessor*. With the exception of Maryland and Montana where assessors are state employees, each taxing jurisdiction appoints or elects its local assessor (Census of Governments, 1992). There is some variability among states regarding how property-taxing jurisdictions are defined. As Table 4.3 indicates, the taxing jurisdictions are commonly defined along county boundaries. It is interesting to note that there

text continues on page 47

TABLE 4.1 Local Property Tax Bases by Property Type, 1991

State	Real Property	Business Inventories	Other Commercial and Industrial	Agricultural	Household Personal Property	Motor Vehicles	Intangible Personal Property
Alabama	P T	E	P T	P T	I T	P T	P T
Alaska	P T	L	L	L	P L	L	E
Arizona	P T	E	P T	T	I T	E	E
Arkansas	P T	T	T	T	T	T	E
California	P T	E	P T	P T	I T	E	E
Colorado	P T	E	T	P T	I T	P T	E
Connecticut	P T	E	P T	P T	E	T	E
Delaware	P T	E	E	E	E	E	E
District of Columbia	P T	E	P T	P T	E	E	E
Florida	P T	E	P T	P T	P T	T	S
Georgia	P T	T	T	P T	E	E	S
Hawaii	P T	E	E	E	E	E	E
Idaho	P T	E	P T	P T	I T	E	E
Illinois	P T	E	E	E	E	E	E
Indiana	P T	T	T	T	I T	E	E
Iowa	P T	E	E	E	E	E	S
Kansas	P T	T	T	P T	I T	S	S

continued

TABLE 4.1 continued

State	Real Property	Business Inventories	Other Commercial and Industrial	Agricultural	Household Personal Property	Motor Vehicles	Intangible Personal Property
Kentucky	P T	T	T	P T	E	T	T
Louisiana	P T	T	T	E	E	E	P T
Maine	P T	E	T	P T	E	E	E
Maryland	P T	L	L	L	E	E	E
Massachusetts	P T	P T	P T	T	E	E	E
Michigan	P T	E	T	E	I T	E	S
Minnesota	P T	E	T	E	E	E	E
Mississippi	P T	P T	T	E	E	T	P T
Missouri	P T	E	T	T	E	P T	S
Montana	P T	E	T	P T	E	T	E
Nebraska	P T	E	T	T	E	T	E
Nevada	P T	E	P T	T	E	E	E
New Hampshire	P T	E	E	E	E	E	E
New Jersey	P T	E	T	E	E	E	E
New Mexico	P T	T	P T	P T	E	E	E
New York	P T	E	E	E	E	E	E
North Carolina	P T	E	T	P T	E	T	S
North Dakota	P T	E	E	E	E	E	S

State							
Ohio	P T	P T	P T	E	E	E	S
Oklahoma	P T	T	T	T	P T	E	E
Oregon	P T	E	P T	E	E	E	E
Pennsylvania	P T	E	E	E	E	E	T
Rhode Island	P T	T	T	P T	P T	T	S
South Carolina	P T	E	P T	E	E	T	E
South Dakota	P T	E	E	E	E	E	E
Tennessee	P T	E	P T	P T	P T	T	P T
Texas	P T	T	T	P T	L	L	S
Utah	P T	E	P T	P T	E	E	E
Vermont	P T	L	P T	E	E	E	E
Virginia	P T	T	T	L	L	T	E
Washington	P T	E	T	T	E	E	P T
West Virginia	P T	T	T	T	T	T	P T
Wisconsin	P T	E	T	T	E	E	E
Wyoming	P T	E	T	T	E	E	P T

SOURCE: Adapted from Census of Governments (1992), Assessed Valuations for Local General Property Taxation, Appendix F.

NOTE: E = exemption; I = taxable only if used in the production of income; L = local option: option to exempt affected items is exercised in most jurisdictions; P = taxable but subject to partial exemptions either specified types or specified value levels; S = subject to special, rather than general, ad valorem taxation; T = locally taxable.

TABLE 4.2 Gross and Net Assessed Value of Property Subject to Local General Property Taxation by Property Type, 1991 (by percentage)

State	Total	State Assessed[a]	Locally Assessed Total	Real Property	Personal Property
United States	100%	4.3%	95.7%	86.9%	% 8.8%
Alabama	100	15.4	84.6	55.6	29.0
Alaska	100	42.4	57.6	50.5	7.1
Arizona	100	22.1	77.9	68.2	9.7
Arkansas	100	9.6	90.4	67.3	23.1
California	100	4.4	95.6	89.5	6.0
Colorado	100	7.5	92.5	82.1	10.5
Connecticut	100		100.0	85.5	14.5
Delaware	100		100.0	100.0	
District of Columbia	100		100.0	95.7	4.3
Florida	100	0.1	99.9	88.1	11.7
Georgia	100	14.9	85.1	70.0	15.1
Hawaii	100		100.0	100.0	
Idaho	100	8.2	91.8	77.5	14.3
Illinois	100	0.2	99.8	99.8	
Indiana	100	5.4	94.6	72.7	21.9
Iowa	100	9.8	90.2	90.2	
Kansas	100	16.3	83.7	66.8	16.9
Kentucky	100	7.9	92.1	69.2	22.9
Louisiana	100	20.2	79.8	44.1	35.7
Maine	100		100.0	89.8	10.2
Maryland	100	15.1	84.9	84.1	0.8
Massachusetts	100	0.4	99.6	97.3	2.3
Michigan	100		100.0	87.7	12.3
Minnesota	100	7.8	92.2	91.3	1.0
Mississippi	100	12.4	87.6	56.9	30.6
Missouri	100	7.0	93.0	72.9	20.1
Montana	100	30.1	69.9	51.9	18.0
Nebraska	100	4.4	95.6	82.0	13.7
Nevada	100	13.0	87.0	77.7	9.3

			Locally Assessed		
State	*Total*	*State Assessed*[a]	*Total*	*Real Property*	*Personal Property*
New Hampshire	100%		100.0	100.0	
New Jersey	100		100.0	99.3	0.7
New Mexico	100	17.9	82.1	77.6	4.5
New York	100	3.4	96.6	96.6	
North Carolina	100	6.4	93.6	73.1	20.5
North Dakota	100	8.3	91.7	91.7	
Ohio	100	20.8	79.2	74.7	4.5
Oklahoma	100	17.7	82.3	64.6	17.8
Oregon	100	5.7	94.3	89.7	4.6
Pennsylvania	100		100.0	100.0	
Rhode Island	100		100.0	83.8	16.2
South Carolina	100	18.0	82.0	55.6	26.3
South Dakota	100	4.8	95.2	95.2	
Tennessee	100	6.6	93.4	84.4	9.1
Texas	100		100.0	79.2	20.8
Utah	100	24.0	76.0	61.6	14.4
Vermont	100		100.0	94.4	5.6
Virginia	100	5.5	94.5	86.1	8.4
Washington	100	3.7	96.3	90.5	5.8
West Virginia	100	12.7	87.3	43.6	43.6
Wisconsin	100		100.0	94.8	5.2
Wyoming	100	71.1	28.9	18.2	10.8

SOURCE: Adapted from Census of Governments (1992), Assessed Valuations for Local General Property Taxation, Table 1.

NOTE: a. State-assessed property refers to property for which the initial valuation for purposes of local property taxation is set by the state, not a local assessor. A large portion state property consists of utility, mining, and oil and gas property.

TABLE 4.3 Taxing Jurisdictions, 1991

State	Taxing Jurisdiction
Alabama	County
Alaska	Borough
Arizona	County
Arkansas	County
California	County
Colorado	County
Connecticut	Borough, city, or town
Delaware	County
District of Columbia	District of Columbia
Florida	County
Georgia	County
Hawaii	County
Idaho	County
Illinois	Municipality or township under county supervision
Indiana	Municipality or township under county supervision
Iowa	County
Kansas	County
Kentucky	County
Louisiana	Parish
Maine	City or town
Maryland	County
Massachusetts	City or town
Michigan	City, village, or township
Minnesota	County
Mississippi	County
Missouri	County
Montana	County
Nebraska	County
Nevada	County
New Hampshire	City or town
New Jersey	Borough, city, town, or township
New Mexico	County
New York	Village, city, or town
North Carolina	County

State	Taxing Jurisdiction
North Dakota	Municipality or township under county supervision
Ohio	County
Oklahoma	County
Oregon	County
Pennsylvania	County
Rhode Island	City or town
South Carolina	County
South Dakota	County
Tennessee	County
Texas	County
Utah	County
Vermont	City or town
Virginia	County or city
Washington	County
West Virginia	City or town
Wisconsin	County or city
Wyoming	County

SOURCE: Adapted from Census of Governments (1994), Assessed Valuations for Local General Property Taxation, Appendix H.

has been little change in the organizational pattern of property tax jurisdictions during the past three decades.

Some types of property are more difficult to value than others. Intangibles such as stocks and bonds pose little problem because their value is reported daily in the financial press. Tangible personal property such as automobiles are usually valued at the current market value. Tangible business property is valued at its book value, that is, its cost less its accumulated depreciation. Depreciation accounts for the decrease in value of the asset—for instance, machinery—over its useful life.

Undoubtedly, the most difficult type of property to value is real property. In theory, the most desirable method of assessing a property's value would be to determine the price that would result from an arms-length transaction between a willing buyer and a willing seller. In other words, the best measure of the value of a property is what someone is willing to pay for it. Unfortunately, the assessor cannot rely on everyone consummating a property sale at the time of valuation. Instead, depending on the type of property, the assessor generally employs one of three valuation methods: *fair market value, capitalization of net income,* or *replacement cost less depreciation.*

Residential Homes

Residential homes are most frequently valued by determining the fair market value of the house on the date of assessment. This is a relatively straightforward valuation method for houses that have recently been sold. But what about homes that have not sold for 20 or 30 years? Again, the process is relatively straightforward. After noting such items as square footage; number of rooms, including bedrooms and baths; and improvements such as swimming pools, sidewalks, and garages, the assessor can identify sales of similar neighboring homes and establish a market value for the residence. This task has been greatly assisted by the use of computers in keeping track of property sales.

Small Business Property

The valuation of residential property is less complex than valuation of property such as small businesses, which are sold infrequently. Because fair market values for small businesses are unlikely to be readily determined, business property is commonly valued by a procedure called capitalization of net income. Capitalization of net income links the value of the commercial property to the profits earned by the business (Odden & Picus, 1992). For example, if the profits of a particular business are $20,000 per year and the expected rate of return on this business is 10%, the value of the property is $200,000 ($20,000/10%). Similarly, the value of a commercial building can be determined by measuring the value of the rents that could be obtained from renting the building. In this case, total rents could be divided by the average rate of return to determine the property's value.

Large Business Property

Determining the value of large commercial enterprises, such as factories is even more complex than valuing small businesses. Capitalization could be used, but it is difficult to allocate profits among segments of the business that are spread across a number of geographic areas (Odden & Picus, 1992). The method of property valuation that is most often used in these cases is replacement cost less depreciation. Replacement cost, as the term suggests, is the cost that would be incurred to replace a factory completely. Using only the replacement cost of the factory, however, would overstate the true value of the property. To account for decreases in value of the factory due to wear and tear, depreciation is calculated. Replacement costs less depreciation represents an estimate of the property's value.

Utility and Railroad Property

Utility property, such as gas and electric lines, and railroad property, such as tracks, pose an interesting set of problems for assessors. Alone, tracks and electric lines that cross a locality are of little value. However, when pieced together, tracks and lines form an enterprise that is of considerable value. States have implemented numerous methods to value utility and railroad property. The most common approach, the *unit rule,* combines aspects of the capitalization-of-net-income and replacement-cost-less-depreciation methods to determine what the value of the entire system is on the valuation date. Portions of the value of the system are then allocated to taxing jurisdictions in which the system is located.

Farmland

The market value or selling price that could be realized from the sale of farmland often exceeds the farming value of the land. This is particularly true for farms in or near growing urban areas. Thus, valuing farmland poses an interesting dilemma for the assessor. If the assessor values the property according to its *highest and best use,* a term often used by assessors, the property would be valued at the fair market value of undeveloped commercial or residential property. If this valuation method is used, however, the farmer would likely be forced out of business. Because of the undesirable effects of such a practice, states commonly provide laws that except actual use as the highest and best use. In general, there are three types of such provisions: *preferential use laws, deferred taxation provisions,* and *provisions for contracts and agreements* (Census of Governments, 1992).

Preferential use laws value property based on its current use (e.g., agriculture), without providing for a tax consequence if the use of the property changes. In 1991, 27 states had such provisions.

Deferred taxation provisions value property based on its current use (e.g., agriculture), as long as the qualifying use continues. If there is any change in use, the property owner is responsible for deferred taxes on the property. For example, if a farmer ultimately sells the property for development purposes, the taxing jurisdiction will collect back taxes, based on the highest and best use valuation of the property prior to sale. In 1991, deferred tax provisions existed in 31 states.

Provisions for contracts and agreements allow taxpayers to contract for a specific period of time during which they agree to use property for certain purposes (e.g., agricultural) in exchange for valuation of the property at other than highest and best use. In 1991, 14 states and the District of Columbia had provisions for contracts and agreements.

Benefit use provisions are also used to value other types of property. For example, a parking lot in an urban area would be expected to have a capitalized income value far below its market value if the property were sold to a developer. Benefit use provisions permit the parking lot to continue its operations without being overly burdened by tax rates determined by the property's highest and best use. As Table 4.4 reveals, many states employ two or three benefit use provisions.

Determining the Assessed Value

Once the value of a property is determined, the next step is to assign an assessed value to the piece. It is the assessed value that becomes part of the property tax base. Each state prescribes the legal standard for all assessed value or a group of standards for different types of property. Assessed value is usually expressed as some percentage of a property's market value. For example, an assessment standard may require property to be assessed at 100% of market value. Market value is also called *full cash value* or *true value in money*. Alternatively, an assessment standard may require property to be assessed at 40% of market value. Table 4.5 presents the legal standards of value for the United States and the District of Columbia.

TABLE 4.4　Benefit Use Provisions by State, 1992

State	Benefit Use Provision
Alabama	Deferred taxation
Alaska	Deferred taxation
Arizona	Use value assessment only
Arkansas	Use value assessment only
California	Use value assessment only Contracts and agreements
Colorado	Use value assessment only
Connecticut	Use value assessment only
Delaware	Deferred taxation
District of Columbia	Contracts and agreements
Florida	Deferred taxation Use value assessment only Contracts and agreements
Georgia	Deferred taxation Contracts and agreements
Hawaii	Deferred taxation Contracts and agreements
Idaho	Use value assessment only
Illinois	Deferred taxation Use value assessment only
Indiana	Deferred taxation Use value assessment only
Iowa	Use value assessment only
Kansas	Deferred taxation
Kentucky	Deferred taxation
Louisiana	Use value assessment only Contracts and agreements
Maine	Deferred taxation
Maryland	Deferred taxation Use value assessment only Contracts and agreements

(continued)

TABLE 4.4 continued

State	Benefit Use Provision
Massachusetts	Deferred taxation Contracts and agreements
Michigan	Use value assessment only Contracts and agreements
Minnesota	Deferred taxation
Mississippi	Use value assessment only
Missouri	Deferred taxation Use value assessment only
Montana	Use value assessment only
Nebraska	Deferred taxation
Nevada	Deferred taxation
New Hampshire	Deferred taxation Use value assessment only Contracts and agreements
New Jersey	Deferred taxation Use value assessment only
New Mexico	Use value assessment only
New York	Deferred taxation Use value assessment only
North Carolina	Deferred taxation
North Dakota	Use value assessment only
Ohio	Deferred taxation Use value assessment only
Oklahoma	Use value assessment only
Oregon	Deferred taxation Contracts and agreements
Pennsylvania	Deferred taxation Contracts and agreements
Rhode Island	Deferred taxation
South Carolina	Deferred taxation
South Dakota	Use value assessment only

State	Benefit Use Provision
Tennessee	Deferred taxation
Texas	Deferred taxation Contracts and agreements
Utah	Deferred taxation
Vermont	Deferred taxation Use value assessment only Contracts and agreements
Virginia	Deferred taxation
Washington	Contracts and agreements
West Virginia	Use value assessment only
Wisconsin	Contracts and agreements
Wyoming	Use value assessment only

SOURCE: Adapted from Census of Governments (1994). Assessed Valuations for Local General Property Taxation, Appendix C.

It is surprising that in many states, assessed value standards are less than 100% of true market values. When property is assessed at some fraction or percentage of its actual market value, *fractional assessment* is said to exist. For example, a residence could have an actual market value of $100,000 but have a recorded assessed value of $50,000, or 50% of full value ($50,000/$100,000).

The existence of fractional assessment is widespread. Fractional assessment can occur by design, as in states where the standard of value is less than 100%, or it can occur as the result of evolving market conditions, especially in the presence of inflation. For example, an assessment that was equal to 100% of market value at the time of valuation may become higher or lower than its true value as time passes. Recall the earlier discussion about the use of recently sold comparable properties to assign markets values. In theory, every time a property is sold, it would be possible to revalue similar properties. However, maintaining up-to-date property values would be a very costly practice.

The preceding explanation suggests that property values start at full market value and then become fractional as time passes. In

TABLE 4.5 Legal Standards of Value for Residential Property

State	Legal Standard	Statute
Alabama	Fair and reasonable market value	Section 40-8-1, Code of Alabama
Alaska	Full and true value	Section 29.45.110, Alaska Statutes
Arizona	Full cash value	Section 42-201.02, Arizona Revised Statutes
Arkansas	20% of true or full market value	Section 26-26-304, Arkansas Code
California	100% of full cash value	Section 69.5, California Revenue and Taxation Code
Colorado	Target percentage	Section 39-1-104, Colorado Revised Statutes
Connecticut	70% of true market value	Section 12-62c, General Statutes of Connecticut
Delaware	True value in money	Title 9, Section 8306, Delaware Code, Revised
District of Columbia	Estimated market value	Sections 47-813 and 47-820, District of Columbia
Florida	Full cash value	Section 193.011, Florida Statutes
Georgia	40% of fair market value	Section 48-5-7, Official Code of Georgia
Hawaii	100% of fair market value	Section 246-10, Hawaii Revised Statutes
Idaho	Market value	Section 63-923, Idaho Code
Illinois	One third of fair cash value	Sections 205/20 and 200/1-55, Illinois Complied Statutes
Indiana	One third of true tax value	Section 6-1.1-3, Indiana Code
Iowa	100% of actual value	Section 441.21, Code of Iowa
Kansas	30% of fair market value in money	Section 79-1439, Kansas Statutes Annotated
Kentucky	Fair cash value	Section 132.190, Kentucky Revised Statutes
Louisiana	10% of fair market value	Article 7, Section 18, Louisiana Constitution

State	Valuation Standard	Legal Citation
Maine	Just value	Title 36, Section 201, Maine Revised Statutes Annotated
Maryland	Phased-in value	Tax Property Section 8-103, Annotated Code of Maryland
Massachusetts	Full and fair cash value	Chapter 59, Section 2A, Annotated Laws of Massachusetts
Michigan	50% of true cash value	Sections 211.10 to 211.34c, Michigan Compiled Laws)
Minnesota	Initially valued at market value	Sections 273.11 to 273.13, Minnesota Statutes
Mississippi	True value, 10%	Article 4, Section 112, Mississippi Constitution
Missouri	True value, 19%	Section 137.15, Revised Statutes of Missouri
Montana	Market value	Section 15-6-131 to 15-6-155, Montana Code Annotated
Nebraska	Actual value	Section 77-201, Revised Statutes of Nebraska
Nevada	35% of taxable value	Section 361.225, Nevada Revised Statutes
New Hampshire	Full and true value in money	Section 75.1, New Hampshire Revised Statutes Annotated
New Jersey	Taxable value, 20% to 100%	Sections 54:4-2.25 and 54:4-2.26, New Jersey Statutes Annotated
New Mexico	One third of market value	Section 7-37-3, New Mexico Statutes Annotated
New York	No standard of value	Section 1802, New York Real Property Tax Law
North Carolina	True value in money	Section 105-283, General Statutes of North Carolina
North Dakota	Residential, 9%	Sections 57-02-01 and 57-02-27, North Dakota Century Code
Ohio	Taxable value, not to exceed 35%	Sections 5715.01 and 5713.041, Ohio Revised Code
Oklahoma	Fair value, not to exceed 35%	Article X, Section 8, Oklahoma Constitution
Oregon	100% of true cash value	Section 308.232, Oregon Revised Statutes
Pennsylvania	Actual value	Title 72, Sections 5020-402 and 5453.602, Pennsylvania Statutes

continued

TABLE 4.5 continued

State	Legal Standard	Statute
Rhode Island	Full and fair cash value	Section 44-5, 12, General Laws of Rhode Island
South Carolina	4% of fair market value	Sections 12-43-220 and 4-9-195, Code of Laws of South Carolina
South Dakota	Taxable value not to exceed 100% of fair market value	Sections 10-4-32 and 10-6-33, South Dakota Codified Laws
Tennessee	25% of fair market value	Section 67-5-801, Tennessee Code Annotated
Texas	Fair market value	Section 26.02, Texas Tax Code
Utah	71% of fair market value	Sections 59-2-102, 59-2-103, and 59-2-201, Utah Code Annotated
Vermont	100% of fair market value	Title 32, Sections 3482 and 3607, Vermont Statutes Annotated
Virginia	Fair market value	Section 58.1-3201, Code of Virginia
Washington	100% of true value	Section 84.20.030, Revised Code of Washington
West Virginia	60% of true and actual value	Sections 11-1c-1, 11-8-5, and 11-8-6, West Virginia Code
Wisconsin	True cash value	Section 70.32, Wisconsin Statutes
Wyoming	Fair market value	Section 39-1-101, Wyoming Statutes Annotated

SOURCE: Adapted from Census of Governments (1992), Assessed Valuations for Local General Property Taxation, Appendix A.

reality, substantial evidence exists that assessed values are intentionally assigned at a fraction of market value. In fact, it has been alleged that fractional assessment practices are used by local assessors to conceal some workings of the property tax. For example, if the practice is to assess property at 50% of market value, the local property taxpayer who owns a parcel with a market value of say $100,000 would receive notice that their property was assessed at $50,000. It is likely that the homeowner would think the house is undervalued; in other words, taxpayers may perceive preferential treatment. If taxpayers think they are being treated preferentially, they are unlikely to complain about their assessed valuations to local assessors. Although they are unlikely to complain, it does not necessarily mean that they are paying less tax. Consider the following example:

	District A	District B
Full value (market)	$100,000	$100,000
Assessed value	$50,000	$100,000
Amount to be raised	$5,000	$5,000
Tax rate	10%	5%

Two districts, A and B, need to raise $5,000 in property tax revenue. Each district has a property tax base whose fair market value is $100,000. District A assesses properties at 50% of fair market value, or $50,000. District B assesses properties at 100% of fair market value, or $100,000. To raise $5,000, District A must tax their base at 10% ($5,000 = $50,000 × 10%), whereas District B must tax their base at 5% ($5,000 = $100,000 × 5%). Therefore, although A's tax base was assessed at a fraction of its fair market value, to raise the required amount of property tax revenue, a higher tax rate had to be levied.

This example highlights how fractional assessment serves to conceal tax differences between districts. Fractional assessments, however, can also hide inequities between taxpayers in the same district. For example, two neighbors with the same $100,000 homes, one with an assessed value of $60,000, the other with an assessed value of $50,000, might both feel they are getting a break when in fact the former has a greater burden. This scenario can result if houses are revalued when property is sold. California, for example, requires that property be revalued on the date of sale. The abrupt increase in assessments and the corresponding increase in tax bill after the sale of the house are sometimes referred to as a "welcome neighbor" tax.

Fractional assessment is a regrettable practice that serves no economic function. In fact, public finance experts argue that property should be assessed at full value or 100% (Odden & Picus, 1992). When property is required by law to be assessed at market value, property or owners are more likely to monitor the system and point out any dramatic differences between assessed values and the potential selling price of their property. Unfortunately, even though the majority of states impose fair market value as their standard of value, the most recently published data suggest that nationally, single-family dwellings are assessed at approximately 44% of market value (Census of Governments, 1982).

The practice of fractional assessment also creates problems across taxing jurisdictions. For example, what if local assessment practices dictate that in District A, all property with full market values of $100,000 be valued at $75,000, whereas in District B, all property with full market values of $100,000 will be valued at $50,000. Such a practice would not necessarily result in inequities within the district (i.e., properties of equal value would be taxed equally). However, states distribute aid to localities based on need, commonly measured by property wealth. Many states, for example, distribute aid to schools inversely with district property wealth. That is, property-poor districts receive more aid than property-rich districts, all else equal. In our example, if each district had a single property, District B, which appears poorer, would receive a larger share of school aid. In this case, equals would be treated unequally.

The product of this scenario is the creation of state equalization rates. Equalization rates are used to convert locally assessed values to full market value to ensure that aid allocations based on property wealth are distributed as intended. In general, state agencies estimate the market value of a sample of property in a local taxing jurisdiction. The estimates of market values are then compared with local assessed values and the equalization rate determined. For example, an equalization rate of 2.0 for District B would convert accurately the assessed property value to full market value (2.0 × $50,000 = $100,000). Unfortunately, the establishment of equalization rates is a complex and difficult task, and few are as precise as in this example. In fact, many states create entire agencies to measure and quantify local assessments for purposes of equalizing property values across taxing jurisdictions (e.g., New York State Board of Equalization and Assessment).

One means of improving the accuracy and effectiveness of assessment administration is to require by law frequent reevaluations of property. Table 4.6 reveals that states vary in their levels of commitment to periodic assessments.

The computer age has made possible annual assessments of property. In particular, computers make possible bulk appraising, at least for residential property, through the use of statistical tools that match comparable properties. It is likely that computer technology will continue to facilitate future advances in assessment practices.

Exclusions From the Property Tax Base

Not all property located within a taxing jurisdiction is assessed and included in the tax base. States and localities have either fully or partially exempted various classes of property from the tax base. Fully exempt property (i.e., property, not included in the tax base) includes the following:

- Property held for nonprofit uses such as religious, educational, charitable, or government property
- Certain economic development property, such as commercial or industrial property, that is exempt to attract business to a taxing jurisdiction
- Property held for environmental purposes, such as property used for pollution control, energy conservation, or property rehabilitation (Census of Governments, 1992)

Many states and localities also grant partial exemptions from the property tax base. These partial exemptions are commonly called *homestead exemptions.* Homestead exemptions provide property tax relief to qualifying elderly, blind, disabled, and veteran homeowners by exempting a portion of their property value from the property tax base. Table 4.7 provides a summary of homestead exemption provisions across the United States.

text continues on page 74

TABLE 4.6 Periodic Assessments

State	Revaluation Period	Statute
Alabama	Assessor has right to assess real estate annually.	Section 40-7-1, Code of Alabama
Alaska	Production of annual roll is required.	Section 29.45.160, Alaska Statutes
Arizona	Annual valuation and listing of each property is required.	Section 42-221, Arizona Revised Statutes
Arkansas	Assessor is required to appraise all real property annually.	Section 26-26-1101, Arkansas Code
California	Assessment rolls are produced annually but valuation changes are limited to 2% annually except for change in ownership or new construction.	Article XIIIA, Section 2, California Constitution
Colorado	Annual listing, appraisal, and valuation are specified.	Section 39-1-105, Colorado Revised Statutes
Connecticut	Municipalities are required to revalue all real property every 10th year.	Section 12-62, General Statutes of Connecticut
Delaware	Preparation of annual assessment roll is specified by statute in each county.	Title 9, Sections 1308, 7004, 8301, Delaware Code, Revised
District of Columbia	Assessment of all realty is required on an annual basis.	Section 47-820, District of Columbia
Florida	Real property is required to be assessed at just value on January 1 each year.	Section 192.042, Florida Statutes
Georgia	Provision is made for opening the books for return of taxes each year.	Sections 48-5-18 and 48-5-263, Official Code of Georgia
Hawaii	Annual preparation of assessment is mandated.	Section 246-44, Hawaii Revised Statutes

State	Provision	Citation
Idaho	20% of property in each specified category must be included in each year's appraisal. This results in complete appraisal of all property every 5 years.	Section 63-221, Idaho Code
Illinois	General reassessment is required in all counties every 4 years.	Chapter 35, Illinois Complied Statutes
Indiana	A general reassessment is required each 4th year.	Title 6, Section 1.1-4-4, Indiana Code
Iowa	Assessment is to occur every 2 years, but assessors may revalue realty whenever a change in value occurs.	Section 428.4, Code of Iowa
Kansas	Provision is made for annual listing and assessment of all real estate as of January 1.	Section 79-1412a, Kansas Statutes Annotated
Kentucky	Annual valuation of each parcel of taxable realty is specified with physical examination no less than once every 4 years.	Section 132.690, Kentucky Revised Statutes
Louisiana	All taxable property must be reappraised at intervals of not more than 4 years.	Article VII, Section 18, Louisiana Constitution
Maine	Physical inspection and inventory of each realty parcel is required at least every 4 years.	Title 36, Section 328, Maine Revised Statutes Annotated
Maryland	In each county, one third of real parcels are reviewed each year, so all are reassessed during a 3-year cycle.	Tax Property Section 8-104, Annotated Code of Maryland
Massachusetts	Fair cash valuation each year is specified.	Chapter 59, Section 38, Annotated Laws of Massachusetts
Michigan	Completion of the assessment role is required annually.	Section 211.24, Michigan Compiled Laws

continued

TABLE 4.6 continued

State	Revaluation Period	Statute
Minnesota	Assessor shall actually view and determine market value of each real property at maximum intervals of 4 years.	Section 273.08, Minnesota Statutes
Mississippi	Land must be assessed annually.	Section 27-35-47, Mississippi Constitution
Missouri	Real estate shall be assessed annually.	Section 137.080, Revised Statutes of Missouri
Montana	Revaluation of all taxable property is required by 1996 and at least every 3 years thereafter.	Section 15-7-111, Montana Code Annotated
Nebraska	A reappraisal of any and all lands and improvements at actual value shall be made when ordered by state tax commissioner.	Section 77-1301.06, Revised Statutes of Nebraska
Nevada	County assessor must reappraise all real property at least once every 5 years.	Section 361.260 Nevada Revised Statutes
New Hampshire	In April of each year, all realty is reappraised if change in value has occurred.	Section 75.8, New Hampshire Revised Statutes Annotated
New Jersey	Annual determination of full and fair cash value of each parcel is required.	Section 54:4-23, New Jersey Statutes Annotated
New Mexico	County assessor must update values to maintain current and correct values of property.	Section 7-36-13, New Mexico Statutes Annotated
New York	All real property, as of March 1 taxable-status date, shall be valued as of the preceding January 1.	Sections 301 and 302, New York Real Property Tax Law
North Carolina	Counties are required to revalue every 4 years.	Section 105-286, General Statutes of North Carolina

North Dakota	All taxable real property shall be listed and assessed every year with reference to its value on February 1.	Section 57-02-11, North Dakota Century Code
Ohio	Reappraisal every 6 years in each county.	Section 5715.33, Ohio Revised Code
Oklahoma	All taxable real property is assessed every year and physically inspected every 4 years.	Article 68, Section 2817, Oklahoma Statutes
Oregon	Real property shall be appraised at least once every 6 years.	Section 308.234, Oregon Revised Statutes
Pennsylvania	Statutes specify annual assessment in counties of the first class and triennial assessments in second-class through eighth-class counties.	Title 72, Sections 5020-401, Pennsylvania Statutes
Rhode Island	Reevaluations must be completed on dates specified by statute for a particular city or town.	Section 44-5- 11, General Laws of Rhode Island
South Carolina	The South Carolina tax commission has the power to order reassessment when in its judgment such assessment is advisable.	Section 12-4-510, Code of Laws of South Carolina
South Dakota	All real and personal property subject to taxation shall be assessed annually.	Section 10-6-2, South Dakota Codified Laws
Tennessee	Reappraisal and equalization is required every 4 or 6 years, as specified by county.	Section 67-5-1601, Tennessee Code Annotated
Texas	Reappraisal of all real property shall occur at least once every 3 years.	Section 25.18, Texas Tax Code
Utah	Assessors are required to visit each district annually.	Section 59-2-203, Utah Code Annotated

continued

64

TABLE 4.6 continued

State	Revaluation Period	Statute
Vermont	On April 1, listers shall take property inventories and personally examine properties to appraise all at fair market value.	Title 32, Sections 4041, Vermont Statutes Annotated
Virginia	In counties, there shall be reassessment every 4 years. In independent cities, there shall be reassessment every 2 years.	Section 58.1-3250, Code of Virginia
Washington	Revaluation requires revaluing all taxable real property within a county at least every 4 years, with physical inspection at least once every 6 years.	Section 84.41.030, Revised Code of Washington
West Virginia	All property shall be assessed annually as of the first day of July at its true and actual value.	Section 11-3-1, West Virginia Code
Wisconsin	Each taxation district is required to assess property at full value at least once every 5 years.	Section 70.05, Wisconsin Statutes
Wyoming	All taxable property shall be annually listed, valued, and assessed for taxation.	Section 39-2-101, Wyoming Statutes Annotated

SOURCE: Adapted from Census of Governments (1992), Assessed Valuations for Local General Property Taxation, Appendix D.

TABLE 4.7 State Property Tax Homestead Exemptions and Credits (Generally, Laws in Effect for 1994)

State	Eligible Homesteaders	Maximum Value of Exemption
Alabama	All	$4,000 AV on state taxes, $2,000 AV on county taxes
	Elderly, blind, and disabled with AGI under $12,000	Total exemption from state taxes, $5,000 AV on county and school district taxes
	Elderly with AGI under $7,500	Total exemption of homestead on all taxes
Alaska	Homeowners 65 and over, widows or widowers 60 and over, or disabled veterans	$150,000 AV
	Renters with identical characteristics as homeowners	
Arizona	Widows, widowers, disabled, honorably dis-charged veterans	$2,340
Arkansas	Disabled veterans, unremarried surviving spouses, and minor dependent children	Entire homestead up to 80 rural acres and 1/4 acre in city
California	All	$7,000 of full cash value if owner-occupied principal residence
	Disabled veterans and dependents	$100,000 AV
	Veterans or unremarried spouses	$40,000 AV
Colorado	Elderly, disabled with income of $7,500 or less	Grant based on payment of taxes
Connecticut	Disabled	$1,000 AV
	Veterans	$1,000 AV
	Disabled veterans and dependents	$1,500-$30,000 depending on disability

continued

TABLE 4.7 continued

State	Eligible Homesteaders	Maximum Value of Exemption
Delaware	Elderly or totally disabled homeowners with annual income of $3,000 or less	$5,000 AV from state or county taxes
District of Columbia	All owner-occupants with not more than five dwelling units	$30,000 AV
Florida	All	$25,000 AV
		Up to value of $500; total exemption for some disabled
Georgia	All	$2,000 AV
	Elderly 62 and over with income less than $10,000	$4,000 AV, $1,000 AV on local education assessment
	Disabled veterans and dependents	$32,500 AV
Hawaii	All	$20,000 AV on owner-occupied principal home
	Elderly	$40,000–$50,000 AV depending on age
	Blind, disabled, and Hansen's disease sufferers	$25,000 AV to full exemption depending on county
	Disabled veterans and dependents	Total exemption if owner-occupied
Idaho	All owner-occupied structures	$50,000 AV or 50% AV, whichever is less, for homestead improvement
Illinois	All owner-occupied residences	$3,500 AV ($4,500 AV in Cook County)
	Elderly owner-occupants	$2,000 AV

State	Eligibility	Benefit
	Disabled veterans with specially adapted housing	$50,000 AV
	Total	$30,000 AV
		Homestead improvement—up to $30,000 increase in AV caused by new improvement for 4-year period
Indiana	All (principal residence and 1 acre surrounding)	Credit of 4% of property tax liability
	Mortgage or contract buyers	Least of (a) balance of mortgage or contract indebtedness, (b) 1/2 total AV, or (c) $1,000
	Elderly with AGI less than $15,000 and real property AV less than $19,000	$1,000 AV
	Blind or disabled with taxable gross income less than $13,000	$2,000 AV
	Veterans	$2,000-$4,000 AV
	WWI veterans, real property AV $24,000	
Iowa	All	$4,850 of actual value; minimum credit of $62.50
	Disabled veterans with income less than $25,000	Full exemption
Kentucky	Elderly and disabled	$6,500
Louisiana	All homesteads not exceeding 160 acres	$7,500 AV
Maine	Estates of veterans aged 62 or 100% disabled and their dependents	WWI veterans $7,000 AV; paraplegics $47,500 AV; other veterans $5,000 AV
	Blind	$4,000 AV

continued

TABLE 4.7 continued

State	Eligible Homesteaders	Maximum Value of Exemption
Maryland	Blind	$6,000 AV
	100% permanently disabled veterans	Total exemption
Massachusetts	All	With city or town approval, 20% of average AV deducted on principal residence
	Elderly (over age 70) owner-occupants with total estate less than $20,000 ($40,000 for communities that have adopted local option statutes) and surviving spouses and minors	$2,000 in value or $175 in taxes, whichever is greater
	Certain veterans, disabled veterans, and dependents	$2,000–$10,000 or $175–$875 in taxes, whichever is greater (depending on disability); paraplegic veterans or surviving spouses receive a total exemption
	Blind	$6,000 in value or $525 ($500 if locally approved) in taxes, whichever is greater
	Elderly with low income or low total estate	Maximum $500
	Paraplegics	Full
	Hardship	Based on assessor's judgment
Michigan	Disabled veterans with specially adapted housing	Total exemption
Minnesota	All	Homestead aid to local governments

Mississippi	All	$5,850 AV–Exemption based on sliding scale amount equal to approximately 40 mills times total AV not to exceed $240
	Disabled and elderly homeowners	$6,000 AV
Montana	Low-income persons with AGI of not more than $12,974 single or $15,569 joint, and residences of totally disabled or deceased veterans with AGI not	$80,000 AV for low-income individuals Total exemption for certain disabled veterans more than $15,000 single or $18,000 jointly
Nebraska	Elderly homeowners	100% of actual value up to $35,000 for household incomes of $10,400 or less
	Disabled	Same as above
	Veteran disabled by a non-service-connected accident or illness	Same as above
	Totally disabled veteran and unremarried surviving spouse	100% of actual value up to $35,000 for household incomes of $15,000 or less
Nevada	Widows, orphans, veterans	$1,000 AV
	Blind	$3,000 AV
	Disabled veterans	$10,000 AV
New Hampshire	Elderly (68 or over) with net assets less than $35,000 and net income less than $5,000 ($6,000 if married)	$5,000 AV (ages 65-75)

continued

TABLE 4.7 continued

State	Eligible Homesteaders	Maximum Value of Exemption
	Blind	$10,000 AV (ages 75-80)
		$20,000 AV (ages 80 or older)
		$15,000 in value
	Disabled veterans and dependents	$50-$1,400 in taxes; total exemption for specially adapted homesteads
New Jersey	Elderly, disabled, and surviving spouses	$250 property tax deduction or rebate
	Veterans	$50 property tax deduction or rebate
	100% permanently disabled veterans	Total exemption
New Mexico	All heads of household	$2,000 AV
	Veterans and unremarried surviving spouses	$2,000 AV
New York	Elderly, veterans, disabled veterans	No general statewide homestead exemption. However, local taxing bodies are authorized to enact certain exemptions.
North Carolina	Elderly or disabled owner-occupants with disposable income not exceeding $11,000	$15,000 AV
	Disabled veterans and dependents	$38,000 AV
North Dakota	Elderly, disabled, disabled veterans with annual income of $15,000 or less	20%-100% reduction in taxable value based on income

Ohio	Elderly, disabled with AGI of $5,200 or less	$1,000-$5,000 of taxable income
Oklahoma	All	$1,000 AV
	Heads of household with gross income $10,000 or less	Additional $1,000 AV
Oregon	Disabled veterans or widows of veterans	$7,500 AV
	Service-connected disabled veterans or widows	$10,000 AV
Pennsylvania	Paraplegic, blind, amputee, disabled veterans or unremarried spouses	Total exemption
Rhode Island	Blind	$6,000 AV
	Veterans	$1,000-$2,000 AV
	Totally disabled veterans	$10,000 AV
	Prisoner of war	$15,000 AV
	Gold Star Parents	$3,000 AV
South Carolina	Elderly, blind, and disabled	$20,000 fair market value
	Paraplegics, disabled veterans, or unremarried spouses	Total exemption of dwelling house and lot (not to exceed 1 acre)
South Dakota	Disabled veterans with specially adapted housing	Total exemption

continued

TABLE 4.7 continued

State	Eligible Homesteaders	Maximum Value of Exemption
Texas	All, elderly, disabled veterans, and disabled	School districts have a mandatory $5,000 homestead exemption. Local option: 20% of appraised value (minimum $5,000) may be offered by any taxing unit. School districts have an additional mandatory $10,000 exemption to those 65 and over or disabled. Local option: at least $3,000 to 65 and over or disabled may be offered by any local taxing unit.
Utah	Disabled veterans, blind veterans or their unmarried surviving spouses or minor orphans	$11,500 taxable value real and personal property
		Veterans' real and personal property, including business property, maximum $30,000 taxable value, based on percentage of disability
	Elderly	$475 homeowner's credit
Vermont	Veterans of American Wars and their widows	$10,000 exemption value of owner-occupied real and personal property; towns may increase amount of exemption to $20,000 under local option
	Veterans with at least 50% disability and their dependents	
	Veterans receiving wartime dependent and indemnity compensation, wartime death compensation, or a pension for disability	

State	Eligibility	Benefit
Virginia	Elderly or disabled owner-occupants with total combined income not exceeding $30,000 and combined net worth (excluding the value of the dwelling and 1 acre of land) not exceeding $75,000	Counties, cities, and towns are authorized to provide deferrals or exemptions of realty taxes
Washington	Elderly (61 and over) and disabled with income restrictions	Special levies: 100% exemption for households with incomes of $26,000 or less Regular levies: income up to $15,000–first $34,000 AV or 50% of total AV is exempt, whichever is more Income $15,001–$18,000–first $30,000 AV or 30% of total AV up to maximum of $50,000 is exempt
West Virginia	Elderly and disabled owner-occupants	First $20,000 AV
Wisconsin	All homeowners	School tax rate times the first $9,150 of value of owner-occupied residential property
Wyoming	All homesteads with AV less than $5,850 but more than $3,900	Credit up to $590
	AV under $3,900	Credit up to $1,460
	Veterans and unremarried widows	$2,000 AV
	Disabled veterans	$2,000 AV times the ratio of the percentage of disability to 100%

SOURCE: Adapted from ACIR (1994). *Significant Features of Fiscal Federalism: Volume 1*, Table 40.

NOTE: AGI = adjusted gross income; AV = assessed value

Property tax exclusions have reached significant proportions. In 1991, for example, the following 12 states reported partial exemptions in excess of 5% of the total gross assessed valuation: Alabama (12.3%), Florida (14.1%), Hawaii (13.4%), Idaho (15.0%), Illinois (7.6%), Indiana (10.6%), Louisiana (27.5%), New York (6.4%), Oklahoma (6.2%), Rhode Island (6.0%), Texas (7.3%), and West Virginia (7.1%; Census of Governments, 1992).

Calculating the Tax Yield[1]

Once the assessed value of a taxing jurisdiction has been established and the amount to be raised determined, it is a simple matter to calculate the required rate of tax. The rate is equal to the amount to be raised, commonly termed the *yield*, divided by the total assessed value (i.e., tax base) of the jurisdiction. The basic formula is as follows:

$$\text{Tax Rate} = \frac{\text{Yield}}{\text{Tax Base}}$$

Or equivalently:

$$\text{Yield} = \text{Tax Rate} \times \text{Tax Base}$$

For example, suppose a school district's tax base is $400 million and it needs to raise $10 million. The tax rate it needs to impose to raise this amount, given its tax base, is equal to $10 million divided by $400 million, or 0.025. In percentage terms, the tax rate can be said to be equal to 2.5%. The tax rate can also be expressed in terms of dollar amounts per certain amount of the tax base (i.e., assessed valuation), such as the following:

25 dollars per 1,000 dollars of assessed value

2.50 dollars per 100 dollars of assessed value

25 cents per 10 dollars of assessed value

2.5 cents per 1 dollar of assessed value

25 mills per 1 dollar of assessed value

Notice that each of the entries in the list describes 2.5% ($25 is 2.5% of $1,000 and $2.5 is 2.5% of $100, etc.). Of all the entries, only the first two and the last one are common in discussions of school finance, and in the latter case, the reference is simply to a tax rate of 25 mills (a mill is an Old English coin that is equal to one tenth of one cent).

Property Tax Limitations

Many states impose a variety of statuary and constitutional limitations that limit abilities of property-taxing jurisdictions to raise revenue. According to the Advisory Commission on Intergovernmental Relations (ACIR; 1995), the most common types of limits are these:

- Overall property tax rate limits that set a ceiling that cannot be exceeded without a popular vote: These limits apply to the aggregate rate of tax on all local governments
- Specific property tax rate limits that set a ceiling that cannot be exceeded without a popular vote: These limits apply to specific types of local jurisdictions (e.g., school districts or counties)
- Property tax levy limits that constrain the total revenue that can be raised from the property tax, independent of the rate
- Assessment increase limits that control the ability of local governments to raise revenue by reassessment of property or through natural or administrative escalation of property values
- Full Disclosure and Truth in Taxation provisions that require public discussion and specific legislative vote before enactment of tax rate or levy increases

As Table 4.8 reveals, there is considerable variation in how states use these limits.

TABLE 4.8 Tax and Expenditure Limits on Local School Districts, 1991

State	Overall Property Tax Rate Limit	Specific Property Tax Rate Limit	Property Tax Revenue Limit	Assessment Increase Limit	General Revenue Limit	General Expenditure Limit	Full Disclosure
Alabama	X	X					
Alaska							
Arizona	X			X		X	
Arkansas		X					
California	X	X		X	X	X	
Colorado		X	X		X	X	X
Connecticut							
Delaware							
District of Columbia							
Florida		X		X			X
Georgia		X					X
Hawaii							
Idaho	X	X					X
Illinois		X	X				X
Indiana			X				
Iowa		X		X		X	
Kansas						X	
Kentucky		X	X				X

State						
Louisiana				X		
Maine						
Maryland	X		X			
Massachusetts						
Michigan	X			X	X	X
Minnesota	X	X				
Mississippi				X	X	
Missouri				X	X	
Montana		X			X	
Nebraska		X			X	
Nevada	X				X	X
New Hampshire						
New Jersey		X			X	
New Mexico			X	X	X	X
New York					X	
North Carolina						
North Dakota				X	X	
Ohio				X		X
Oklahoma						X
Oregon				X	X	X
Pennsylvania						
Rhode Island						

continued

TABLE 4.8 continued

State	Overall Property Tax Rate Limit	Specific Property Tax Rate Limit	Property Tax Revenue Limit	Assessment Increase Limit	General Revenue Limit	General Expenditure Limit	Full Disclosure
South Carolina							X
South Dakota		X					
Tennessee							
Texas		X	X				X
Utah		X					
Vermont							
Virginia							
Washington	X		X				
West Virginia	X	X	X				X
Wisconsin					X		
Wyoming		X					

SOURCE: Adapted from the Advisory Commission on Intergovernmental Relations (ACIR) (1995) Table 1, page 5.

Final Comments

Assigning value and levying property tax is a complex task. This discussion merely presented an overview of the common valuation methods for select classes of property. Readers interested in more detailed discussion of property valuation procedures are encouraged to contact the property tax assessors in their state or local taxing jurisdiction.

Note

1. This discussion draws directly from Monk (1990).

FIVE

DOES REFORMING THE
PROPERTY TAX MAKE SENSE?

The presumption throughout this chapter is that although the real property tax has shortcomings, it is still a viable option for financing schools if revised in a number of alternative ways. Several distinct reform strategies will be examined. First, the focus will be on reforming a number of administrative practices within the existing system. Here, the strategy will be to maintain the property tax at the local level while making a number of minor (although not necessarily easy to implement) administrative reforms. Second, there is an examination of mechanisms designed to address the regressive features of the property tax, including circuit breakers and reverse equity mortgages. Third, the focus shifts to more ambitious reform strategies that entail reorganizing or consolidating local districts. Fourth, and last, attention will be given to proposals that expand the local tax base for purposes of financing public education.

Administrative Reforms

Chapter 4 suggested that states vary greatly with regard to the structure and administration of their property tax systems. Indeed, it is common for states to differ in these respects:

- The boundaries along which property tax jurisdictions are defined
- The types of property subject to taxation

- The manner in which properties are assigned value
- The legal standard that defines assessed value
- The acceptable level of variation within property classes
- The level of commitment to periodic assessments
- The provisions that specify the fraction of property that will be excluded from the tax base
- The statutory and constitutional provisions that limit the jurisdictions' ability to raise property tax revenues

Although the specific features of a state's property tax system vary, in theory, the policies selected should produce a system that is essentially fair and easily understood by taxpayers. To accomplish this goal, the system needs to rest on an appropriate administrative foundation. Unfortunately, the property tax is arguably the most difficult tax to administer. Other broad-based taxes, such as the tax on income, require that the taxpayer make the determination of the taxes owed. On the other hand, property tax systems require that the tax liability be determined by the administrative unit on a parcel-by-parcel basis. To best accomplish this task, several practices of "good" property tax administration have been recommended. Among the key features are the following (Berne & Netzer, 1995):

- The specification of a legal standard of value and the valuation of the parcel that matches the legal standard

In the majority of states, the legal standard is market value or some fraction of market value. Therefore, so-called good practice requires the assessor to determine market value and then apply the percentage to convert the property's value to taxable assessed value. States vary in their commitment to how often current market values are determined. For example, some require all parcels to be revalued once every 3 or 4 years. Others require infrequent reassessment cycles, such as once every 10 years. Best practice is considered annual revaluation (Berne and Netzer, 1995).

- Good property tax administration requiring that assessors take advantage of the economies of scale that accompany larger organizational structures

Many states administer the property tax at the county level rather than smaller government units. The county administrations help mitigate inconsistencies in the level of training provided to assessors that often accompany smaller units. Similarly, administering the property tax at the county level allows assessors to take advantage of the knowledge and experience required to assess hard-to-value property, including most nonresidential property. In fact, in several states, major classes of commercial and industrial property are valued at the state level. Moreover, in the majority of states, public utility and transportation carrier property, such as railroads, are valued by a state agency (Berne and Netzer, 1995).

- Equalization needed for the implementation of statewide policies, including school aid calculations and for the determination of individual tax liabilities when parcels are located in more than one taxing jurisdiction

The equalization process should be understandable to taxpayers and produce results that do in fact equalize properties across jurisdictions. Because there are fewer units to equalize, larger taxing jurisdictions make it easier to perform interjurisdictional equalizations. Therefore, good administrative practice recommends that the county level be the minimum unit for equalization.

- Most important, good administrative practice requiring that the property tax system be easily understood by taxpayers

Provisions outlining tax preferences, such as homestead exemptions, should be simplified to ensure that eligible taxpayers can take advantage of these options. Similarly, individual property tax bills and assessment rolls should clearly specify the steps taken to convert the initial determination of market value to taxable value. For instance, the record for any property should identify these four figures (Berne and Netzer, 1995):

1. The market value determined by the assessor
2. That value times the standard value percentage specified by law
3. The amounts of any partial exemptions (e.g. homestead exemptions)
4. The net taxable value

Providing taxpayers with an easily understood report detailing how their property tax liability is calculated could restore the public's confidence in the property tax system. Indeed, much of the public discontent with the system stems from the perception that the property tax is being poorly administered. In response to these concerns, many property tax jurisdictions have taken broad steps to improve public relations. For example, the Churchill County Assessor's Office, Fallon, Nevada, has gone so far as to provide property taxpayers with a "Bill of Rights." The bill reads as follows:

As a property taxpayer you possess certain rights. You have the right:

to an Assessor's Office with an "open door" policy

to a just and equitable assessment of your property, conducted in accordance with Nevada Statutes and regulations of the Nevada Tax Commission

to prompt and courteous attention from the Assessor's Office whenever you have a question concerning any aspect of your appraisal

to complete details that set forth the Assessor's procedures for assessing your property, including a copy of your appraisal records

to appeal to the County Board of Equalization, the State Board of Equalization and the court system if you feel your appraisal is incorrect

to a notice in the newspaper informing you the year your property is reappraised

to have the Assessor's Office be an advocate to the Legislature on behalf of taxpayers

to an Assessor's Office that disseminates new laws and information to the public through the media and speaking to civic groups

to an appointment with the appraiser who appraised your property for a review of your assessment

to be advised by the Assessor's Office of all your rights as a taxpayer (Kroft, 1995)

Whereas recommending that property tax jurisdictions adopt and enforce a taxpayer's Bill of Rights may be extreme, the benefits that accompany a well-administered property tax system are evident. First, establishing a clear standard of value contributes to uniformity in the administration of the property tax. Second, frequent reevaluations can prevent inconsistencies in the treatment of properties produced by fractional assessments. Third, larger administrative units can take advantage of scale economies in training and offset the difficulties associated with establishing equalization rates in smaller jurisdictions. Fourth, and most important, a properly administered and easily understood system can restore the public's confidence in the property tax as a viable source of school district revenues.[1]

Targeted Tax Relief

Implementation of the administrative practices just described can reduce many of the perceived shortcomings of the property tax. However, additional steps need to be taken to directly address what is perhaps the most regrettable feature of the property tax, the regressive nature of the tax's impact on residential property. Recall that a regressive tax is one in which tax burdens rise as income levels fall. That is, poorer households devote a greater percentage of their income to paying property taxes relative to wealthier households. This phenomenon contributes much to the controversy and public concern surrounding the use of the property tax to support schools.

In an attempt to remedy this perceived shortcoming of the property tax, many states have implemented targeted tax relief mechanisms to reduce the property tax burdens faced by low-income individuals. Targeted tax relief mechanisms may be classified in two broad groups: homestead exemptions and circuit breakers. Homestead exemptions, the oldest form of property tax relief, usually take the form of a percentage or dollar reduction in the assessed valuation of real property held by eligible taxpayers (e.g., elderly). For example, in Texas, school districts are required by law to exempt $10,000 of assessed value for homeowners that are 65 and over or disabled.[2]

Circuit breakers, on the other hand, derive their name from the following analogy. They (circuit breakers) are designed to protect taxpayers against property tax "overload" in the same manner an electrical circuit breaker protects a power line against an overload of current. Overload may be the result of a drop in current-year income due to illness, unemployment, or other extraordinary circumstances.

Overload may also be the result of a drop in income due to retirement. Circuit breakers provide payments to taxpayers, usually in the form of income tax credits, equal to the excess residential property tax liabilities over a designated percentage of income. Table 5.1 provides an overview of circuit breaker programs and their eligibility requirements by state.

Prior to 1963, no state provided residential property tax relief through circuit breakers. Currently, all but a handful of states offer some sort of circuit breaker program. It is interesting to note that many circuit breaker programs also include poor and elderly renters. These provisions recognize that property taxes are commonly passed on to tenants in the form of higher rents.

Because the programs differ in design, eligible households, and benefits, they lead to varying property tax reductions and levels of effectiveness. For example, it is common for states to grant relief only to elderly or disabled homeowners. Circuit breaker programs with age restrictions and disability provisions, however, do little to provide tax relief for ineligible, poor homeowners. In addition to age, most states also include income criteria in determining eligibility for circuit breaker relief. As Table 5.1 indicates, these limits are quite varied, as are the maximum benefits granted.

Although circuit breakers offer many poor and elderly taxpayers relief from their property tax burdens, it is important to highlight the extent to which this is accomplished. Table 5.1 reveals that the average level of benefits granted in the states that reported these figures ranges from $593 (Maryland) to $80 (California), with a median of $257 (Pennsylvania). These findings suggest that states vary greatly in the generosity of their programs. It is interesting that New York, a state that consistently ranks among the highest with regard to property tax burdens, reported an average benefit of only $93 per household. New York's circuit breaker program, therefore, is unlikely to be successful at reducing the burden of the property tax on low-income individuals.

The relative success of circuit breaker provisions are not only dependent on the scope of the program but also on the ability of eligible taxpayers to take advantage of the option. Recall that good property tax administration requires that the property tax system be easily understood by taxpayers. This includes provisions outlining tax preferences, such as circuit breakers. Unfortunately, findings suggest that circuit breaker programs are severely underused by eligible

text continues on page 91

TABLE 5.1 Circuit Breaker Programs by State, 1994

State	Eligibility	Property Tax Equivalent for Renters	Income Ceiling	Maximum Benefit	Average Benefit
Alabama	No state programs				
Alaska	No state programs				
Arizona					
Homeowners	Age 65+		$3,750/$5,000	$502	$266
Renters	All	5% of rent	$25,000	$40	$38
Arkansas					
Homeowners	Age 62+		$15,000	$250	$118
Renters				96% of tax	
California					
Homeowners	Age 62+		$24,000	Payment of first $30,000 full value	$80
Renters	Disabled, blind	$250			
Colorado					
Homeowners	Age 62+		$7,500/$11,200	$500	$336
Renters	Disabled, blind	20% of rent		$500	
Connecticut					
Homeowners	Age 65+, disabled		$19,400/$23,000	$1250	$450
Renters	Age 65+, disabled	35% of rent		$900	$385
Delaware	No state programs				
District of Columbia					
Homeowners	All		$20,000	$750	$300
Renters	All	15% of rent	$20,000	$750	
Florida	No state programs				
Georgia	No state programs				

	Eligibility		Income		
Hawaii					
Homeowners	All		$30,000	$50	$49
Renters			$15,920	$600	$284
Idaho					
Homeowners	Age 65+, disabled		$14,000	$780	$272
Renters					
Illinois					
Homeowners	Age 65+, disabled		$10,000	$140	
Renters	Age 65+, disabled	30% of rent			
Indiana					
Homeowners	Age 65+, disabled		$12,000	$1,000	$251
Renters					
Iowa					
Homeowners	Age 65+, disabled		$17,200	$600	$196
Renters	Age 65+, disabled	27.5% of rent			
Kansas					
Homeowners					
Renters		15% of rent			
Kentucky	No state programs				
Louisiana	No state programs				
Maine					
Homeowners			$8,400/$10,500	$400 elderly, $3,000 nonelderly	$369 elderly, $352 nonelderly
Renters		15% of rent			
Maryland					
Homeowners				Unlimited	$593
Renters		15% of rent		$600	$278

continued

TABLE 5.1 continued

State	Eligibility	Property Tax Equivalent for Renters	Income Ceiling	Maximum Benefit	Average Benefit
Massachusetts	No state programs				
Michigan					
Homeowners	All		$82,650	$1,200	$503
Renters	All	17% of rent			
Minnesota					
Homeowners	All		$60,000	$400	$290
Renters	All		$35,000	$1,000	
Mississippi	No state programs				
Missouri					
Homeowners	Age 65+		$15,000	$750	$262
Renters	Age 65+			$750	
Montana					
Homeowners	Age 62+			$400	$236
Renters	Age 62+	15% of rent		$400	
Nebraska	No state programs				
Nevada					
Homeowners	Age 62+		$19,100	$500	$210
Renters	Age 62+	8.5% of rent		$500	
New Hampshire	No state programs				
New Jersey					
Homeowners	All		$100,000	$500	
Renters	All	18% of rent		$500	

State / Category	Eligibility	% of rent	Income limit	Benefit	Benefit
New Mexico					
Homeowners	Age 65+		$16,000		$141
Renters	Age 65+			$250	$250
New York					
Homeowners	All		$18,000		$93
Renters	All	25% of rent		$375 elderly / $75 nonelderly	
North Carolina	No state programs				
North Dakota					
Homeowners	Age 65+, disabled		$13,000	$400	$3,170
Renters	Age 65+, disabled	20% of rent		$230	$95
Ohio					
Homeowners	Age 65+, disabled		$16,500		$199
Renters					
Oklahoma					
Homeowners	Age 65+, disabled		$10,000	$200	$117
Renters					
Oregon					
Homeowners	Age 58+		$10,000		$560
Renters				$2,100	
Pennsylvania					
Homeowners	Age 65+, disabled		$15,000	$500	$257
Renters	Age 65+, disabled	20% of rent			
Rhode Island					
Homeowners	Age 65+, disabled		$12,500	$200	$170
Renters	Age 65+, disabled	20% of rent			
South Carolina	No state programs				
South Dakota					
Homeowners	Age 65+, disabled		$9,000/$12,000		$145
Renters					

continued

TABLE 5.1 continued

State	Eligibility	Property Tax Equivalent For Renters	Income Ceiling	Maximum Benefit	Average Benefit
Tennessee					
Homeowners	Elderly, disabled		$8,200		$89
Renters	No state programs				
Texas	No state programs				
Utah					
Homeowners	Age 65+, disabled		$17,325	$450	$450
Renters					
Vermont					
Homeowners	All		$45,000		$518
Renters	All	24% of rent			
Virginia	No state programs				
Washington	No state programs				
West Virginia					
Homeowners	Age 65+, disabled		$5,000		
Renters	Age 65+, disabled	12% of rent			
Wisconsin					
Homeowners	All		$19,154	$1,450	$425
Renters	All	25% of rent			
Wyoming					
Homeowners	Age 65+, disabled		$10,000/$14,000	$630 single, $723 married	$521
Renters					

SOURCE: Adapted from Lankford and Wyckoff (1995), Appendix 1. See also ACIR (1994), Significant Features of Fiscal Federalism, Volume 1, Table 39.

taxpayers. For example, reports estimate that fewer than half of all of those eligible for the New York State circuit breaker credit actually file for one (Lankford & Wyckoff, 1995). If states are to ensure that eligible taxpayers take advantage of these options, they should take steps to simplify the application process and conduct an awareness campaign to enhance participation.

Reverse Equity Mortgages

As has been pointed out in this and the previous chapter, it is possible for people with relatively low current incomes to have substantial property holdings. Many circuit breaker programs treat these individuals preferentially, even though they are more able to pay than someone with the same current income who lacks substantial property holdings. In these cases, circuit breaker programs do not address the regressivity of the property tax but rather, its illiquid nature. An alternative approach has emerged in recent years that addresses the problem faced by "property rich and cash poor" taxpayers. These programs are commonly referred to as reverse equity mortgages (REMs).

Reverse equity mortgages are designed to allow the elderly to convert the accumulated equity in their homes into an income stream, without having to move or sell their property interests. Generally, the borrower receives a monthly payment from the lender, to be repaid with interest either on the borrower's death, the sale of the house, or at a fixed repayment date. The difference between an REM and a traditional mortgage is that in the former, each disbursement by the lender reduces the homeowner's equity interest. Although numerous variations of REMs are offered by both the public sector and banking industry, these instruments may be divided into four broad classes (Scholen, 1992):

1. *Fixed-term reverse mortgages.* The lending institution will disburse to the homeowner a monthly advance, generally calculated on 80% of the appraised value of the home for a predetermined period (generally 3 to 10 years). On completion of the designated term, the loan principal, plus interest, must be repaid in full.

2. Tenure reverse mortgages. The lending institution will disburse to the homeowner a monthly advance, as determined by the assessed value of the property and the life expectancy of the borrower (determined actuarially), until such borrower dies, moves, or sells the residence. On the occurrence of any of the aforementioned events, the borrower, or his or her estate is required to pay the loan balance in full.

3. Line of credit reverse mortgages. This instrument is designed to allow borrowers to draw a flexible amount of equity if, when, and to the degree that it is required. The amount of the line of credit is determined by the life expectancy of the homeowner and the assessed value of the designated property. The loan balance will be repaid in full on the relocation or death of the borrower or the sale of the residence.

4. Shared appreciation mortgages. Under this type of arrangement, a variation on all three of the types of reverse mortgages, the lender agrees to provide the borrower with a larger monthly payment (or credit line) in exchange for a future share in the property's appreciation. However, when you die, move, or sell the residence, you or your estate are required to remit to the lender the agreed-on portion of your home's appreciation, plus the balance of your monthly advances (including interest).

The first REMs appeared on the scene in 1961. For several decades, however, the banking industry failed to aggressively pursue the promotion of the debt instrument. The lending industry's hesitancy was largely due to the fact that no secondary market existed for the selling or securing of executed loans. In other words, lending institutions were required to manage the entire risk of their REM portfolios, hardly desirable for a product that had yet to demonstrate its earnings potential. In 1988, however, Congress established the Home Equity Conversion Mortgage Insurance Demonstration, the first federal endorsement of home equity conversion (HECM) as a viable option for the elderly. By 1992, Congress had expanded the number of HECMs that the Department of Housing and Urban Development (HUD) could insure from 2,500 to 25,000.[3] In addition, Fannie Mae, as part of its 1992 $10-billion affordable-housing initiative, committed to purchase the HUD-insured HECM loans, thereby creating a secondary market for originators who do not want to maintain and continually fund HECM loans in their own portfolios.[4]

Since the federal government's endorsement of REMs, lending institutions have aggressively marketed the debt instrument. However, personal investment and retirement publications are generally split on their support for the REMs. Among the advantages and disadvantages commonly listed are the following:

Advantages:

- The borrower retains title to the property. Therefore, the homeowner maintains possession of the residence until death or voluntary disposal.

- The proceeds of the loan can be used for any purpose, including satisfying housing expenses, such as taxes, insurance, and fuel, or general living expenses, such as food and health care.

- The loan advances are a return of equity and not income; therefore, the transaction is not a taxable event. Therefore, the inflow of funds will not have an adverse effect on the receipt of other supplemental programs, such as Medicare or social security.

Disadvantages:

- Because title to the property is retained by the homeowner, the borrower is responsible for the taxes, repairs, and maintenance of the residence. These property-related expenses are likely to increase, whereas the monthly payment remains fixed.

- The liquidation of the property interest will presumably diminish the estate of the borrowers and accordingly, the eventual distribution to their heirs.

- The interest on the obligation is not deductible until the loan is satisfied in full.

- As in a traditional forward mortgage, several fees arise during the origination of the REM. For example, the homeowner is responsible for appraisals, title search and insurance, inspections, recording fees, servicing fees, and any other professional costs, such as accountant's and attorney's fees. In addition, lenders charge an *origination fee* for arranging the mortgage, generally expressed as a percentage of the home's value or the amount of equity being mortgaged. Many insured lenders also charge "risk" premiums ranging from 2% to 7% of the house's value. Like points on a traditional mortgage, the premiums are charged on origination.

- Under all obligations, interest is charged.

The demand for REMs has been limited. This may be the result of the public's perception that the mortgages are too costly (fees and interest). Or, it may be that seniors are understandably reluctant to touch the equity nest eggs they have taken their entire lives to build. Equally plausible is that the notion of "house rich-cash poor" elderly citizens is not truly reflective of the economic reality of the aged. Indeed, studies have found that most low-income elderly have very little housing wealth (Venti & Wise, 1991). In other words, those who are most likely in need of property tax relief, the poor, do not have the equity to liquidate. In short, the ability of REMs to address problems inherent in the property tax system, namely its illiquid nature, is questionable.

District Consolidation

Following the earlier tradition of educational decentralization established in New England, the U.S. common-school movement of the 19th century established tax-supported, locally controlled schools intended to serve community interests. The process resulted in the formation of thousands of local school districts throughout the United States. By 1930, the number of school districts exceeded 127,000 nationwide (Swanson and King, 1997).

The common-school movement did much to promote educational opportunity among the nation's many school children. However, the creation of education systems that were largely dependent on local revenue sources did little to ensure equality in the resources devoted to schooling. Beginning in the late 19th century, many states attempted to equalize the resources available to students by combining smaller, independent districts into larger ones. This effort, commonly referred to as the consolidation movement, resulted in the elimination of thousands of one-school districts. The first districts to consolidate were located in cities. In 1897, for example, over 350 districts merged to form one educational system in New York City. Widespread consolidation of rural schools occurred after improved means of transportation became available in the mid-20th century. By 1994, only 14,708 school districts remained (Center for the Study of States, 1995).

District consolidation, also called reorganization, is the joining of two or more districts to form a single, larger district. Arguments in favor of the school district consolidation are of two general types: equity and efficiency. The equity argument focuses on the notion of equal educational opportunity. If some children are denied an appropriate education because they reside in districts with small, inadequate schools, they have been denied equal educational opportunity. The efficiency argument, on the other hand, focuses on costs. If economics of scale are present, it will cost more to produce the same services in smaller schools than in larger ones. Often, reforms combine these two views when arguing for district consolidation.

Despite such lofty claims, it is unclear whether consolidation efforts do in fact promote the goals of equal opportunity and efficiency. In fact, in a comprehensive study of a statewide district reorganization plan, Monk and Haller (1986) raise doubts about the efficacy of the policy option.[5] Examining district consolidations in New York State, Monk and Haller first looked at the equity argument. The authors posited that if district consolidations promote equality in educational opportunity, the policy change should have a positive impact on student achievement, student social development, and program comprehensiveness. In regard to the first two aspects of equity, Monk and Haller found no compelling evidence to support the state's policy promoting school reorganization. In fact, students of smaller schools performed better on standardized tests and had more opportunities for social development (e.g., participation in extracurricular activities) than students of larger schools. In reference to the third aspect of equity, program comprehensiveness, the authors did find evidence that smaller schools offer fewer courses. In particular, districts with secondary schools of less than 400 students appeared to be unable to offer the variety of programs available to students attending larger secondary schools. However, once high schools serve this number of students, further increases are not associated with enhanced program offerings, a substantial number of students do not seem to take advantage of them either.

Monk and Haller (1986) next turned their attention to the second argument for consolidation, efficiency. Recall that the efficiency argument rests on the notion of economies of scale. That is, larger schools can offer a given program at a lower unit cost than smaller schools. For example, it costs less per pupil to teach a science course to 25 students than to 10. Although Monk and Haller acknowledged that economies of scale are possible, they found no compelling evidence that increased efficiency is routinely served by school district consolidation. In fact, the authors point to the possibility that consolidation efforts can produce diseconomies of scale. That is, increased costs associated with larger school systems may outweigh the cost savings realized when schools consolidate.

School district consolidation remains a popular policy option despite the uncertainties surrounding the existence of scale economies in education. In fact, New York State provides substantial operating and building incentive aids for districts willing to merge.[6] Despite these fiscal enticements, however, district consolidation in New York has slowed to a virtual halt. One explanation is that district consolidation, ever unpopular, has become a less salient option as the debate continues on the optimal size, increased student benefits, and savings realized when districts consolidate. Equally plausible, the decline is a reflection of the fact that there are significantly fewer districts to consolidate and the most workable consolidations have already taken place.

In summary, there is no conclusive evidence that either equality of educational opportunity or increased efficiency will as a matter of course result from district consolidation. It follows, then, that there is no justification for states to offer substantial financial incentives to districts willing to merge or to otherwise pursue broad-based consolidation initiatives. It is important to recognize, however, that equity and efficiency may be served by consolidating in particular instances—that is, in the case of a particular set of school districts. The findings reported suggest only that the state's desire to promote equity and efficiency in its schools is not predictably furthered by consolidation efforts. That is, when state officials or policymakers urge the consolidation of two or more districts, they should not assume that the resulting district will be able to offer more and better services at a lower cost. Instead, a comprehensive study of the districts in question should be performed to determine the potential impact of the merger on equity and efficiency objectives. Unfortunately, such studies are not routinely done.

Expanded Tax Base Approaches to School Finance

In addition to consolidation efforts, a number of other policy changes aimed at altering the local property tax base has been proposed in recent years. Among the recommended alternatives is the use of a political or geographical unit larger than the school district as a base for school property taxation. These financing options are commonly referred to as expanded tax base (ETB) approaches. Unlike consolidation efforts, under ETB approaches, participating districts maintain their administrative identity and are treated as a single unit for property tax purposes only.

ETB approaches to financing public schools is a seemingly straightforward solution to problems that accompany smaller tax bases. In fact, the public finance literature is replete with benefits believed to accompany larger tax bases. For example, many argue that ETBs ameliorate the distorting effects the property tax has on the location decisions of firms. All else being equal, firms have an incentive to locate in areas where property taxes are low. Therefore, statewide or regional taxation of businesses for education purposes removes a potential distorting influence and allows location decisions to be made on the basis of real resource costs, such as labor and accessibility to markets, not property tax burdens.

A second argument for ETB approaches to school finance is that these plans limit fiscal competition for economic development among neighboring jurisdictions. Local districts possess the authority to grant property tax abatements as a means of encouraging economic development in their jurisdictions. Abatements exempt certain business properties from taxation, thereby reducing the yield of the property tax for purposes of financing public services, such as education. For example, New York State provides three local-option tax exemption programs for business property. In 1988, these programs exempted over $10 billion of property from taxation (State Board of Equalization and Assessment, 1992). Expanding the local property tax base does not discourage economic development but rather deters ill-advised fiscal competition across local districts for limited business investment. In fact, because individual jurisdictions share in the economic growth of the state or region as a whole, there are incentives for local governments to work together in attracting business.

A third argument for expanding local property tax bases emerges from the fact that governmental, charitable, religious, and educational properties are typically exempt from taxation. Although one may argue that this policy produces societal benefits, these exemptions place burdens on local taxing jurisdictions. In fact, because exempt property tends to be geographically concentrated, this phenomenon imposes disproportionate burdens on taxpayers in jurisdictions with high proportions of exempt property relative to taxable property. Moreover, it is troubling to note that local discretion is generally absent in granting exempt status. For example, in New York, three quarters of allowable exemptions are state mandated, representing 86% of the state's total exempt value (Mullen, 1990). Expansion of the property tax base mitigates the disadvantage faced by jurisdictions whose boundaries contain relatively high proportions of exempt property.

A fourth argument favoring ETB proposals is that expansion of the tax base insulates jurisdictions from the adverse effects of deterioration of the local property tax base. For example, the loss in property tax revenues due to the closing of an industrial plant would be born proportionally by local districts in the state or region in which the firm was located. Absent the ability to share the loss, local jurisdictions would be forced to raise tax rates to maintain existing service levels. This practice can be particularly damaging to the economic well-being of local jurisdictions. For example, studies have demonstrated that an increase in local property tax burdens leads to a reduction in the size of the local tax base (e.g., Ladd & Bradbury, 1988). This results from either of two phenomena. High property taxes may reduce the size of the tax base either by decreasing the level of business or residential activity in the district or by causing property values to decline. If a district continually seeks to raise needed revenue by increasing the local tax rate, the potential for future revenues will be offset by a decrease in the taxable base. The aggregation property at the state or regional level for tax purposes limits the ability of individual jurisdictions to tax themselves out of the market.

A fifth argument for ETB approaches to school finance is that expansion of the tax base limits the ability of local districts to export property tax burdens. Tax exporting refers to the shifting of tax burdens by a locality to nonresidents. For example, when a district taxes commercial, utility, or industrial property, a portion of the properties' taxes can be shifted to nonresident taxpayers in the form of higher output prices, lower wages, or decreased dividends. Depending on the degree of shifting, individuals that acquire goods or services outside their jurisdiction indirectly support another's public services. The possibility of tax exporting can provide incentives for local districts to modify their tax and expenditure policy (Gold, 1994).

A sixth, less recognizable yet important, argument favoring expansion of the local property tax base is that it affords officials the opportunity to improve assessment and valuation practices. As discussed earlier, systematic differences in assessment of properties within and among jurisdictions are common. Expansion of the property tax base to the state or regional level permits administrative units to implement uniform standards and take advantage of economies of scale and emerging technologies.

The most compelling argument for expanding the local property tax base, however, is that such an approach produces a more equitable distribution of a state or region's aggregate property wealth for purposes of supporting public services such as education. In the case of education, both students and taxpayers are believed to benefit from expanded local tax bases. Students benefit because the approach mitigates the primary cause of spending differences, the unequal tax-raising capacity among local school districts. Taxpayers benefit because pooled local tax bases provide a means to equalize tax burdens that support these educational services.

ETB approaches to school finance take two general forms. The first, termed *nonresidential ETB approaches,* permits school districts to maintain taxing authority over its residential property while removing nonresidential property from the local tax base. The pool of nonresidential property is instead taxed at the state or regional level, the proceeds of which are distributed back to local districts in an equalizing manner. The second, *termed comprehensive ETB approaches,* does not draw a distinction between residential and nonresidential property. Instead, a district's entire tax base is taxed at the state or regional level, the proceeds then distributed back to local districts in an equalizing manner.

Comprehensive ETB Approaches

Comprehensive ETB approaches to school finance tax all property within the state or region at a uniform rate. The proceeds are then distributed back to local districts in an equalizing manner. For example, the pooled property tax revenues could be distributed back to local districts in inverse relationship to district wealth measures, such as income or property values. That is, poorer districts would receive a greater share of the pooled property tax revenues relative to wealthier districts. These proposals should not be confused with education finance plans, commonly found in the southeast, where district boundaries are defined by county lines (e.g., Alabama, Florida, Maryland). The defining characteristic of comprehensive ETB proposals is that districts maintain their administrative integrity.

Currently, no state employs a *statewide* comprehensive ETB approach to school finance. Texas, however, recently adopted a school finance plan that, in part, offers districts the option of implementing a *regional* comprehensive ETB plan. Senate Bill 7, designed to reduce spending inequalities among districts, requires high-wealth school districts to take action to lower their property wealth. According to the bill, a district whose property wealth exceeds a state-established ceiling level must exercise some combination of the following options to achieve the targeted wealth level: (a) consolidate with another district, (b) detach property from the district and annex it to another district, (c) purchase attendance credits from the state, (d) contract for the education of nonresident students, or (e) make arrangements for tax base consolidation with another district (Clark, 1995). Whether districts will choose to exercise option (e), a comprehensive ETB approach, and the impact it will have on promoting equity among districts is presently unclear. The constitutionality of Senate Bill 7 was affirmed in early 1995 by the Texas Supreme Court. At the close of 1995, none of the affected districts opted to consolidate tax bases with another district. No other state provides local support for school through regional taxing units.

Although there may be only a single operational example of a comprehensive ETB approach, this school finance plan has also been examined empirically. In a study prepared for the New York Task Force on Equity Excellence in Education, Lamitie, Glasheen, and Bentley (1981) investigated the effects of financing public schools with a state-mandated property tax, its receipts distributed within the county where they were raised. The findings reported by Lamitie et al. suggest that the plan was successful at promoting equalization in spending and taxing patterns at the county level. This was particularly true in counties where there were vast differences in district wealth. In counties where there was little variation in district property wealth, changes in expenditure levels and tax rates were considerably more modest. In a related study, Dembowski and Kemmerer (1984) also reported that comprehensive ETB approaches to school finance have the double benefit of minimizing the relationship between district wealth and spending while equalizing district tax efforts for support of educational programs.[7]

Although the research base is limited, the findings reported suggest that comprehensive ETB approaches to school finance promise to close the gap in spending and tax burdens across districts while producing a variety of collateral benefits believed to accompany larger tax bases.

Nonresidential ETB Approaches

Nonresidential ETB approaches to school finance permit school districts to maintain taxing authority over its residential property while removing nonresidential property from the local tax base. Nonresidential property includes vacant land, commercial, industrial, utility, and agricultural property. The pool of nonresidential property is then taxed at the state or regional level and the proceeds distributed back to local districts in an equalizing manner.

Certain features of nonresidential ETB proposals cause them to be politically and economically more palatable than their comprehensive counterparts. For example, comprehensive ETB approaches move the primary local funding source (i.e., property tax) to a regional or state level. One understandable concern is that an increase in state or regional presence will foster greater regulation of school policies and administration—a result held by many as undesirable. In addition, unlike comprehensive ETB approaches, nonresidential ETB approaches permit school districts to maintain taxing authority over their residential property, thereby preserving a degree of local fiscal control. The theory behind vesting communities with a degree of local fiscal control is that they will be more responsive to educational needs if given the means to express their support. Similarly, in the absence of a clearly defined connection between the tax burden and the educational benefits to be secured, continued support for school funding may be adversely affected. That is, local taxpayers are likely to perceive the social desirability of securing resources for their own schools but may be more resistant to personal property taxes that are collected by the state or region and then redistributed to schools outside their proximate location. To preserve the benefit-burden connection in the voter's mind, local control over residential wealth is held to be desirable.

Whereas fiscal control over residential property may make non-residential ETB proposals more politically palatable than their more comprehensive counterparts, the efficacy of this policy change does not rest exclusively on the degree to which the public is likely to embrace the reform strategy. Rather, the impetus behind this reform strategy is to close the gap between spending and tax burdens across districts. By providing local districts access to larger pools of nonresidential tax revenues, nonresidential ETB proposals promise to accomplish this task. It is interesting that there are no states that rely on nonresidential ETB approaches to school finance.

A handful of studies have emerged, however, that explore the efficacy of nonresidential ETB approaches to school finance. The classic study of this approach was conducted in the early 1970s by Helen Ladd. Ladd (1976) undertook to determine whether a policy change that provided for the statewide taxation of commercial and industrial property for education would in fact improve student and taxpayer equity. The specific policy proposal under examination was the substitution of a metropolitanwide, uniform rate of taxation of industrial and commercial property in the Boston area for the existing local taxation of these properties for education. Ladd developed two separate grant formulas to distribute the revenue raised from the metropolitan tax back to the local districts. The first distributed money to districts solely on the basis of pupil counts (i.e., flat grants). Under the second alternative, the share received by each district varied directly with the number of students and inversely with the residential wealth per pupil. In other words, property-poor districts would receive a larger share of the pooled nonresidential property tax revenues than wealthy districts, all else being equal.

The findings reported by Ladd (1976) suggest that nonresidential ETB proposals would have adverse effects on the pattern of expenditures and tax burdens across districts in the Boston area. Ladd's study produced the following results: In the case of the flat grant per pupil, the relationship between school spending and property wealth increased. That is, the nonresidential ETB approach increased the likelihood that wealthy districts would spend more than their poorer counterparts. In addition, under the flat grant per pupil, the range of expenditures between the highest-spending and lowest-spending districts increased. The second distribution mechanism faired only slightly better; again, the range of expenditures among districts increased.

In 1995, Ladd reexamined the efficacy of a statewide, nonresidential ETB approach to school finance, this time focusing on New York State (Ladd & Harris, 1995). Acknowledging the importance of how the pooled nonresidential property tax revenues are distributed to local districts, the authors developed and tested four distribution formulas. The first two were identical to the ones employed in Ladd's (1976) study. The third distributed pooled revenues to 75% of districts with the lowest residential wealth per pupil. The fourth distributed pooled revenues to 75% of districts with the lowest income per pupil.

The results reported by Ladd and Harris (1995) suggest that under the first alternative, the flat grant per pupil, the proposal did little to improve equity. Under the more equalizing alternatives (i.e., 2, 3, 4), the policy change made the overall distribution of spending across districts somewhat more equitable. However, Ladd and Harris were quick to point out that New York City stands to lose significant amounts of revenue under these funding approaches, whereas rural and suburban districts gain large amounts of external revenue; in effect, already underfunded New York City becomes poorer. In short, the policy change would lead to highly undesirable consequences for the majority of the state's schoolchildren.

In contrast to Ladd (1976) and Ladd and Harris's (1995) efforts, findings reported by Stark (1992) suggest that statewide taxation of nonresidential property stimulates greater tax and spending equity among districts. Simulating the effects of statewide taxation of nonresidential properties for schools in Indiana, Stark concluded that statewide nonresidential ETB approaches to school finance would close the gap in spending and tax burdens across districts.

Evidenced by the limited number and sometimes contradictory studies that have examined this reform strategy, it is clear that there is much to be learned about the efficacy of nonresidential approaches to school finance. In fact, there are no studies that explore the efficacy of *regional* nonresidential ETB proposals. Ladd and Harris's (1995) study demonstrates that the policy change works differently in dissimilar types of districts. Therefore, it is possible that nonresidential ETB proposals of smaller scales will promote student and taxpayer equity across districts.

Although some progress has been made toward understanding ETB approaches to school finance, serious gaps in the knowledge base remain. In fact, studies provide only first approximations of the potential effects of these proposals on measures of student and taxpayer equity. This is an important step forward but falls short of the kind of definitive analysis policymakers would prefer before committing themselves to ambitious reform agendas. Of course, it is always possible to do more research and to have more thorough studies, and a balance needs to be struck between the need to know more and the need to resolve pressing problems.

Final Comments

It should be stressed that the reforms discussed are not mutually exclusive. Indeed, improvements in the administration of the property tax is, in some respects, the most fundamental and far-reaching because it is a prerequisite for success with any of the property tax reform options. In addition, the options are ordered roughly in terms of their relative levels of ambition and departure from many current school finance systems. This is not to suggest that reforms of real property tax administration will be easy to accomplish in any real sense. However, policymakers need to recognize that the property tax is in place and that alterations of its structure represent larger interventions than a relatively straightforward tightening of administrative procedures.

Notes

1. For a comprehensive review of issues of property tax administration, readers may refer to the International Association of Assessing Officers' (IAAO; 1990) *Property Appraisal and Assessment Administration.* For a wide-ranging text that discusses the basic concepts in valuation and tax policy as seen by the courts, refer to

Joan Youngman's (1995) *Legal Issues in Property Valuation and Taxation: Cases and Materials.*

2. Homestead exemptions were explored in detail in Chapter 4 and will not be revisited here.

3. To be eligible, the borrower must be at least 62 years of age, live in a single-family residence, and own the residence free and clear (or nearly so). In addition, the maximum amount of the insurable mortgage is limited by statute. In 1992, the allowable amount, which addresses demographic characteristics of the locality, ranged from $67,500 to $124,875. The primary advantage of these instruments to lenders is that the institution will be protected by HUD if the loan's outstanding balance exceeds the value of the property on the date of sale.

4. Readers interested in comprehensive discussion of REMs can turn to Ken Scholen's (1992) *Retirement Income on the House.*

5. This discussion has been adapted from Monk and Haller (1986).

6. Reorganization incentive aid in the mid 1980s included 20% additional Operating Aid (phased out over 15 years) and 30% additional Building Aid (Monk & Haller, 1986).

7. Dembowski and Kemmerer (1984) studied the effects of the use of comprehensive ETB models for financing schools in the Mohawk Valley Region of New York State.

SIX

SHOULD WE SHIFT AWAY
FROM THE LOCAL PROPERTY TAX?

Education policymakers, public officials, and taxpayers continue to challenge school finance structures that rely heavily on the local property tax for fiscal support. A system that is dependent on the property wealth of a district is alleged to permit wide disparities in per-pupil spending, which in turn foster inequities in educational opportunities and tax burdens across communities. In response to these challenges, education policymakers have entertained numerous proposals that seek to decrease reliance on the local property tax. The more widely espoused remedies include the use of alternative local taxing mechanisms such as income and sales taxes; shifting primary funding responsibility to the state level; and use of nontraditional taxes such as lotteries. In this chapter, we describe these education finance reform efforts and consider their consequences.

Local Income and Sales Taxes

In recent years, many education finance reformers have made a case for abandoning (or significantly reducing) the local property tax in favor of a local income tax. Many of the arguments in favor of shifting to local income taxes look to the framework for evaluating taxes described in Chapter 3. For example, advocates put forth these arguments (e.g., Strauss, 1995):

- A local income tax can be structured to make education taxes more progressive (i.e., fair).

- A local income tax would be more responsive to changes in the economy. For example, if the economy is growing and wages are rising, a local income tax would produce higher revenues without requiring changes in tax rates. In contrast, if property taxes are to keep up with inflation, assessments and tax rates need to be increased every 2 or 3 years. Dramatic changes in property tax rates and assessments can be unsettling to taxpayers and adversely affect the ability of districts to secure revenues.

- The administrative and compliance costs associated with income taxes are less than those that accompany property taxes.

- Although no tax is embraced, the income tax tends to earn greater public acceptance than the property tax.

- The benefit standard dictates that local incomes taxes are a more appropriate source of revenues for schools than property taxes. According to the benefit standard, property taxes should be used only to finance public services directly connected to housing and the maintenance of property. For instance, services such as police and fire protection are examples where the value of a taxpayer's property is a good indicator of the need for public services. That is, taxpayers with extensive property holdings should pay more for fire and police services than taxpayers with modest holdings, and a tax on property gives rise to this result. On the other hand, because schools benefit people rather than property, local income taxes are more appropriate for financing this service than local property taxes.

- Tax on real property does not properly address a taxpayer's ability to pay. Here, the contention is that discrepancies can exist between the value of housing, and accordingly property tax levies, and current income streams. Again, visions come to mind of elderly homeowners on fixed incomes unable to meet their escalating property tax obligations. Local income taxes, which are directly tied to the inflow of resources during a given period, are viewed as an appropriate alternative for low-income taxpayers.

Before we abandon the local property tax, it makes sense to take a closer look at the arguments posed. First, there are a number of desirable features of the property tax. For example, property taxes are generally believed to be more stable sources of revenues that either income or sales taxes. School districts, it is argued, require the stability afforded by reliance on local property tax revenues; shifts to less stable income taxes could make budgeting difficult and place educational programs at risk.

Second, a desirable feature of the property tax (at least from the perspective of some individual school districts) is the opportunity it offers to export taxes to nonresidents. Although from a broad perspective this is not necessarily a desirable feature, from an individual school perspective, the ability to tax nonresidents who own vacation homes can be very attractive. A local income tax, for example, would significantly reduce a school district's access to these revenue streams.

Third, reliance on local income taxes in lieu of property taxes would result in a considerably larger share of the tax burden being borne by local homeowners. This is because the nonresidential portion of the property tax base is usually much higher than its share of the income tax base. For instance, nonresidential property often accounts for 35% to 50% of the total assessed value of property, whereas businesses pay a much smaller percentage of income taxes (Gold, 1994).

It is also difficult to argue that the property tax is completely divorced from ability-to-pay considerations. Although it is true that discrepancies can exist between taxpayers' income and property wealth, there is no question that taxpayers with larger property holdings have greater abilities to pay compared with taxpayers with lesser property holdings, all else being equal. Although it may be difficult for the taxpayer with large holdings relative to current income to pay property taxes, there is no denying that property contributes to an individual's financial well-being.

In addition, it is important to recognize that all local income taxes are not alike. In fact, their structure can greatly influence the ability of the tax to improve equity (i.e., fairness) and administration. Consider the following three working examples (Gold, 1994):

1. In Pennsylvania, local school districts are able to impose up to a 1% local wage tax and are entirely responsible for its administration and collection. Unlike the state and federal income tax, it does not tax dividends, interest, or capital gains (pas-

sive income). Because passive income tends to comprise a larger share of income for the wealthy and because these taxes are levied at a flat rate, Pennsylvania's local income tax is regressive.

2. In Ohio, local school districts receive revenues from a state-administered local income tax applied to the state's taxable income at a flat rate. Because Ohio's taxable income is calculated by subtracting personal exemptions, the tax is only slightly progressive.

3. In Maryland, school districts benefit from a county income tax, which is levied as a percentage of state income tax liability. Because the state income tax is progressive, so is the local income tax.

Of the three examples, the Ohio and Maryland models are preferable. In these states, revenues are collected at the state level; therefore, local governments are not required to create new agencies to administer the tax. More important, because they include passive income, they tend to be at least slightly progressive rather than regressive (Gold, 1994).

The preceding discussion highlights the debate surrounding the use of local income taxes for purposes of financing public schools. However, this debate is best informed by distinguishing clearly between two important features of a local tax: (a) the basis on which it is levied (e.g., property, income, and sales) and (b) the degree of variation in fiscal capacity that is geographically linked. The criticisms outlined earlier focused on the former and not the latter consideration. That is, a tax on income is a more appropriate basis than a tax on property for purposes of financing education. Many complaints about the property tax, however, are due to the fact that it is a *local* tax.

Local tax bases give rise to inequalities in the resources available to districts and the tax burdens required to support educational services. The disparities, however, are not the result of the local property tax but rather reliance on local tax bases. The practical import of this distinction is that a shift from a local property tax to a local tax of some other kind will not solve problems stemming from the local nature of the tax. In fact, empirical studies have demonstrated that a shift from the local property tax to a local income tax does not solve the equity problems that result from the unequal distribution of wealth among districts within a state (Strauss, 1995). In fact, these findings suggest that in the absence of an ambitiously equalizing program of state aid, a local income tax would give rise to unequal levels of spending just as is presently the case with the local property tax.

Much of the analysis of local income taxes also applies to local sales taxes (Gold, 1994). Like the property tax, the sales tax base is distributed unequally across districts. Some districts have access to large pools of commercial property, whereas others have very little. Unlike income taxes, sales taxes are regressive. Policymakers should exercise caution when advocating that a regressive tax be used to finance public services such as education.

Shifting Funding Responsibility to the State Level

In Chapter 1, we noted that the state share of education spending has declined steadily since the mid-1980s, whereas the local share has increased during the same period. Although these figures represent national trends, several states have experienced shifts in the primary funding source for public education from the local to the state level. Increases in state support for schools can result from any or all of the following three events:

1. Courts may rule that the existing school finance system is in violation of the state's education clause. For example, in *Abbott v. Burke*,[1] the court ruled that the New Jersey school finance system was not "thorough and efficient" as guaranteed by the State's constitution. The decision mandated that the state increase education spending in the poorest 28 districts up to the level of spending in the wealthiest districts and that the state provide additional funds to low-achieving students in city districts (Odden & Picus, 1992). Within 2 months, the New Jersey legislature redesigned the school finance structure and greatly expanded the state's role in financing public schools.
2. The state's role in financing public education may also increase as a result of the outcomes of gubernatorial or legislative elections. For example, in the 1980s, New York's governor believed that the state should play the leading role in the fi-

nancing of its public schools. Accordingly, with the support of the legislature, the state's share of education funding rose steadily during this period.[2]

3. The state's share of school funding may also increase as a result of property tax limitation movements. As noted in Chapter 4, many states limit the amount of revenues that can be derived from local property taxes. As a result of placing caps on the amount of revenue that can be raised at the local level, the state often responds by increasing its share of total revenues.

Of particular interest to those of us who wish to understand the changing role the property tax plays in school finance are the increases in state support prompted by tax limitation movements.[3] The *tax limitation movement* may be defined as the recent drive toward legislative and constitutional mandates that reduce or eliminate the local property tax as a source of district revenues. It is interesting that prior to 1976, no state had provisions that limited the aggregate tax or expenditure levels of schools. New Jersey was the first to establish expenditure limits for schools. By 1978, voters in 11 states would pass tax and expenditure limits, with 7 of these limits being constitutional (Kearney, 1995).

In 1978, the tax limitation movement gained national prominence with California's passage of the now infamous Proposition 13. Proposition 13 limited the combined property tax of local governments (cities, counties, schools, community colleges, and special districts) to 1% of the property's full market value. A year earlier, the average property tax rate on a personal residence was 2.6% (Kearney, 1995). Proposition 13 also limited property tax assessment increases to no more than 2% per year, with property reappraised to current market value only when sold, transferred, or newly constructed. The immediate effect of Proposition 13 was to reduce total property tax collections by approximately $7 billion. To compensate for the local revenue lost, the state appropriated its budget surplus. For all intents and purposes, California became a state-funded system, assuming 85% of the cost of public education (Kearney, 1995).

Much has been written about Proposition 13 over the years: the reasons for its passage, consequences for homeowners and businesses, and its fiscal impact on the state and education system (e.g., Picus, 1991). What is important for our purposes is that the lost revenues did not come from new taxes or rate increases on existing taxes but rather from a budget surplus generated by California's growing economy (Kearney, 1995). However, in the 1980s, when California's economy slowed down, the decline in state-generated revenues placed considerable fiscal pressure on California's public schools. Remember, the primary sources of state revenues are from income and sales taxes. Although these revenue sources are highly responsive to economic growth, they are not stable sources of revenues.

The shift of primary funding responsibility to the state level also created other fiscal problems for California's schools. In particular, schools now had to compete with other state services, such as health and welfare, for a share of the state's shrinking resource pool. To ensure that education received a fair share of state resources, in 1988, Californians passed a measure that guarantees that school districts receive a minimum of 40% of the state budget (Proposition 98). This move was hailed by education interest groups as a means to solve the school system's financial difficulties (Picus, 1991). It has come as a surprise, however, that the legislature has treated the spending floor as a spending ceiling and consistently allocated the remaining 60% of the general fund to other services. As a result, there are those who argue that Proposition 13 has resulted in a general reduction in resource levels for California schools (e.g., Picus, 1991).

Following California's adoption of Proposition 13, several other states passed property tax and spending limitations of their own. For example, in 1980, Massachusetts voters approved Proposition $2\frac{1}{2}$. Proposition $2\frac{1}{2}$ required tax jurisdiction with high tax rates to reduce property taxes by at least 15% annually until the rate reached 2.5% of fair market value (Kearney, 1995). Once this level was reached, property taxes could not be raised by more than 2.5% annually. Because the legislature did not provide replacement revenues for the lost property tax revenues, school spending decreased dramatically during the early years of Proposition $2\frac{1}{2}$ (Ladd & Wilson, 1985). In the late 1980s, with Massachusetts experiencing a upturn in the economy, the legislature did appropriate funds to offset the revenue shortages initially generated by Proposition $2\frac{1}{2}$. However, by 1991, fiscal pressures had reduced the state's share to 37%. It is interesting that support for Proposition $2\frac{1}{2}$ was not necessarily a vote for reductions in school spending levels. Rather, the favorable vote reflected concerns over high and growing tax burdens (Ladd & Wilson,1985). In any case, Proposition $2\frac{1}{2}$ provides another example of the potential vulnerability of local schools to statewide property tax limitations.

The most recent example of the property tax limitation movement occurred in Michigan. In July of 1993, the Michigan legislature eliminated the local property tax as a source of district revenues. This action resulted in a loss of $6.5 billion dollars of funding for K-12 education. Later actions by the Michigan legislature and the state voters did replace the lost revenues through a series of provisions. The highlights of the Michigan reform are as follows (Kearney, 1995):

- An increase of two percentage points in the state sales tax (from 4% to 6%)

- A decrease in the local property tax from an average of 34 mills to a state-mandated levy of 6 mills on all property and a local levy (if authorized by voters) of up to 18 mills on non-homestead property

- The opportunity for high revenue districts to levy additional millage to maintain or increase modestly their prior year spending levels

- The opportunity for all districts to levy an additional millage of up to three mills, with voter approval

Although it is early, evidence suggests that the net short-term effects of these reforms include a 4% increase in overall funding, a substantial shift in funding responsibility from the local to the state level (the state share increased from 33% to 79%), and a substantial shift from reliance on the local property tax (the property tax share dropped from 66% to 32% percent; Kearney, 1995).

To best understand the impact of Michigan's reform initiatives, these efforts need to be viewed in light of Michigan's state of affairs in 1993. Prior to 1993, there was a substantial imbalance among the three broad-based taxes that support education. For example, property and income taxes per person were 30% and 38% *above* the national average, respectively. And sales taxes per person were 30% *below* the national average. In other words, the property and income taxes were overused, whereas the sales tax was underused (Kearney, 1995). Policy makers need to keep the Michigan context in mind as they evaluate the relevance of these reforms. Several states, such as

Arizona, New York, and Wisconsin, rank high across all three major tax instruments.

Perhaps because of the widespread media attention that followed Michigan's finance reform efforts, the property tax limitation movement appears to have gained momentum in recent years. For example, the 1994 elections saw no fewer than 10 states with tax and revenue limitations, assessment caps, and plans for property tax reductions (Kearney, 1995). As the foregoing discussion makes clear, state-initiated reforms are quite successful in limiting reliance on the local property tax as a source of district revenue. There is also evidence to suggest that these reforms can reduce interdistrict disparities in spending and tax burdens. For example, as a result of Proposition 13, spending differences across districts have decreased dramatically throughout the state. Moreover, disparities in tax burdens across districts have been all but eliminated (Picus, 1991).

But what are the costs of tax limitation movements? Because the burden of education financing has been placed on the state, local residents and school boards can no longer decide how much to spend on their local schools (unless they desire to reduce spending below the cap). The state's increased presence in fiscal and administrative matters has also been unsettling to advocates of local control. Perhaps more distressing, however, is the fact that of the three states examined (California, Massachusetts, and Michigan), Michigan was the only state that replaced lost revenues. In the other states, no specific actions were taken by the legislatures either to enact new taxes, raise rates, expand bases, or earmark existing taxes. In these cases, the reduction of property taxes has translated into increases in the state share but decreases in the overall level of funding for public schools.

Lotteries

Let us begin by stating that the lottery is a tax. It is of no consequence that individuals play the games voluntarily. It is also of no consequence that a select few will benefit greatly from playing if they are among the lucky winners. Lotteries generate revenues that can be used by governments to finance public services such as education. Perhaps the lottery can be more clearly viewed as a tax if we consider the following example. An individual cannot be coerced into ordering a meal in a restaurant, yet he or she will pay a sales tax. If the individual chooses his or her meal properly, it is highly likely that he or she will benefit from eating it. If the individual chooses poorly and derives little or no benefit, he or she still must pay a sales tax on the purchase. In much the same way the sales tax is levied on the purchase of goods, the lottery is a tax on playing a game.

In 1964, New Hampshire became the first state to use a lottery to help finance public services. In fact, New Hampshire was not only the first state to introduce lotteries but also the first to earmark the revenues for a specific purpose–education (Borg, Mason, & Shapiro, 1991). The new revenue source was not viewed as a means to increase school spending but rather a way to slow down increasing local property tax rates.

In 1968, New York followed suit, also earmarking the proceeds of the lottery for education. In both states, tickets cost several dollars, players needed to register to participate, and drawing took place only a couple of times a year. It should not be surprising that early returns from the lottery were disappointing. In 1971, however, New Jersey introduced several changes that would make lotteries highly successful sources of revenue. Among the innovations were low-priced tickets, instant winners, and aggressive promotional campaigns to increase sales. By 1992, 37 states and the District of Columbia had introduced lotteries, with 12 of them earmarking the proceeds for public education (ACIR, 1994).

Today, lottery proceeds for most states are not derived from a single lottery but from a host of available games, each with features designed to attract players. For example, there are "instant game" tickets where the players scratch off numbers to see if they have won a prize; there are "daily numbers" games where players select a series of numbers, usually three to five, with the winning numbers drawn later in the evening; there are "lottos" where players again select a series of numbers with the winning numbers drawn weekly or biweekly. Lotto prizes are the by far the largest of the games, with players sometimes winning in excess of $100 million. And, most recently, five states have introduced "video lottery terminals" (VLT), which resemble slot machines found in casinos (Swanson & King, 1997). Some argue that VLTs will be the fastest growing lottery game (see also Jones & Amilfitano, 1994).

In 1992, nine states reported revenues in excess of $1 billion: California, Florida, Illinois, Massachusetts, Michigan, New Jersey,

New York, Ohio, and Pennsylvania (ACIR, 1994). Florida's lottery was the greatest revenue producer, reporting in excess of $2 billion dollars. In several states, the proceeds from lotteries accounted for as much as 4% of total budgeted revenues. In short, for the states that implement lotteries, they have proven to be a significant source of revenues. However, before we accept lotteries as an appropriate school revenue source, it is important to examine lotteries in reference to the framework for evaluating taxes introduced earlier.

Equity

Most authors conclude that lotteries are regressive sources of revenues (see Borg et al., 1991). That is, poorer individuals are more likely to devote a greater percentage of their income to playing lotteries than wealthier individuals. Intuitively, this makes sense. The appeal of the lottery is that if you win, you will be rich. If you are already rich, you have less incentive to play. It is interesting that how regressive the lottery is depends on the type of game being played. For example, evidence suggests that instant-winner games are more likely to appeal to the less educated and minorities. Because these groups are more likely to have lower incomes, instant games are highly regressive (Borg et al. 1991). On the other hand, lottos tend to become less regressive as the pot grows. This is because as the prize increases, those of higher-income groups who might not otherwise have played increasingly purchase tickets. In fact, there are those observers who suggest that with very large lotto pots, the tax is proportional or even slightly progressive (see Mikesell, 1989). These findings are significant because the greatest percentage of lottery proceeds are derived from lotto games.

Efficiency

Do lotteries prompt individuals to change their behavior? To answer this question, consider what happens when there is no lotto winner and the pot is carried forward to the next drawing. Even casual observation reveals that it is common for the pot to more than double. For example, Florida recently reported that a lotto jackpot rose from $6 million to $13 million to $27 million to $56 million in 4 consecutive weeks (Borg et al., 1991). Because the lotto pot is based on the number of tickets sold, this finding suggests that individuals are enticed into playing the lottery as the pot grows. Therefore, it appears that lotteries do have the potential to alter individual behaviors.[4]

Scholars have also been able to uncover how the lottery alters the spending habits of households. For example, Borg et al. (1991) report that since the Florida lottery's debut, lottery households have reduced their spending on alcohol by almost $5 per month. The authors also suggest that lower-income households have significantly reduced their utility expenses and reduced slightly their grocery expenses due to the lottery. On the other hand, higher-income households have reduced slightly the amount of money expended for personal grooming. These findings reinforce the belief that lotteries place greater burdens on lower-income relative to higher-income households.

Economic Responsiveness and Stability

Although lotteries have the potential to produce large amounts of revenue, they are also unstable. In general, following the first year of introduction when interest is high, the revenues from lotteries usually taper off. For example, revenues from Pennsylvania's lottery rose 98% in the years immediately following its inception but rose only 4.5% a decade later (Odden & Picus, 1992). Elsewhere, declines have been reported ranging from –1% to –50% (Mikesell & Zorn, 1986). These findings explain why states continually advertise and seek to develop new lottery games to attract players.

Administration and Compliance

The cost of compliance for taxpayers is virtually zero. Indeed, there are no forms to fill out, complicated regulations to interpret, or accountants to hire. On the other hand, compared with other revenue sources, the lottery is very costly to administer. First, vendors usually receive 5% of sales. Second, there are costs for printing tickets, holding drawings, and maintaining the computer system that records lottery sales and entries. These costs can average as high as 5% of sales. In addition, there are the costs of promotion, which average about 1.5% of sales revenue. And last, but certainly not least, a large portion of the revenues is distributed to the winner, up to 50% in most states. Therefore, for every dollar of lottery revenue collected, that state retains only 35 to 40 cents (Borg et al., 1991).

Public Acceptance

Ignoring the moral and ethical issues that surround legal forms of gambling, the lottery is generally accepted as a means to raise revenues for public services, including education. No doubt contributing to this feeling of goodwill is the fact that many do not even realize the lottery is a form of taxation.

Proponents of lotteries argue that the education revenues generated from their use outweigh their shortcomings as tax instruments. The strength of this argument rests on the belief that lotteries enhance or add to the resources available to school children. Unfortunately, the results of several studies indicate that this is not the case. In fact, even lottery revenues earmarked for education have not been found to supplement existing revenues. Instead, these studies suggest that lottery dollars replace previously allocated resources and do not increase spending on education (e.g., Borg et al., 1991). These findings, along with their poor performance on the measures described earlier, cast considerable doubt on the efficacy of lotteries as a source of school funding.

Final Comments

Education policymakers and concerned citizens continue to challenge school finance systems that rely heavily on property taxes as a source of district revenue. In response, several states have implemented far-reaching reforms that have prompted movements away from the local property tax. As the discussion makes clear, like the property tax, many of the options have shortcomings. For example, school finance systems that are dependent on local income and sales taxes do not mitigate the inequities that result from the unequal distribution of wealth across districts. States that assume primary funding responsibility for schools often experience decreases in the overall levels of spending. And it appears that lotteries are not only regressive sources of revenue but do not enhance the level of district spending. The lesson to be learned from the discussion is that education policymakers should exercise caution before they adopt a policy option that abandons or significantly decreases reliance on the local property tax as a source of district revenues. It is possible that the devil you don't know is worse than the devil you know.

Notes

1. *Abbott v. Burke*, 100 N.J. 269, 495 A. 2d 376 (1985), administrative law opinion rendered, EDU 5581-85 (Aug. 24, 1988), slip opinion decided by the Commissioner of Education (Feb. 22, 1989).

2. The outcome of the recent gubernatorial election, in which the successful candidate ran on a tax-reduction platform, suggests that primary responsibility for funding public schools in New York will shift back to local districts.

3. Readers interested in the legal issues that surround school finance court decisions can turn to *School Finance: A Policy Perspective* (Odden & Picus, 1992). For a useful guide in understanding the political process that influences school finance, see *School Finance: Its Economics and Politics* (Swanson & King, 1997).

4. For a comprehensive discussion of lottery tax efficiency, see Borg et al. (1991).

SEVEN

WHAT OTHER WAYS ARE THERE TO RAISE REVENUES?

It is becoming increasingly difficult for schools to provide the educational services demanded by relying exclusively on the proceeds of broad-based taxes such as the local property tax. These difficulties arise in part from recent tax limitation efforts at both the state and local levels and in part from pressures to increase the level of educational services for special needs and at-risk students. In response to this challenge, school districts and in some cases, individual schools have identified alternative and often nontraditional sources of revenue. These efforts can be divided roughly into six categories: user fees, school partnerships, donations, educational foundations, volunteerism, and returns on investments of school resources.

User Fees

User fees represent fees charged by the district to students or nonstudents for the provision of services or the use of facilities. User fees are justified based on the benefit standard discussed earlier. That is, those students or groups that benefit from the use of school facilities or services should pay for these privileges. The practice of assessing user fees to support school activities has proven to be a rather contentious issue, and in this section, we report on what is currently known.

Student User Fees

In states where student user fees are permitted, charges can be assessed for the following:

- Activities, such as field trips and athletics
- Supplies, such as textbooks, art supplies, and towel rentals
- Services, such as before-school and after-school programs, lunches, summer school, elective courses, and transportation

Depending on the nature of the activities, supplies, or services subject to user fees, the charges can be quite varied. For example, fees for supplementary texts and supplies may amount to less than $10 per student. On the other hand, school districts have reported charging user fees in the amount of $1,000 for a technical studies course, $1,500 for extracurricular activities, $110 for graduation fees, and $12,000 for an international program (Swanson & King, 1997).

The practice of shifting the burden of payment from taxpayers to students has in many cases prompted legal challenges. The primary issue is whether fees may be charged for educational services that are guaranteed by state education clauses to be free and available to all children regardless of their socioeconomic status. In response to these claims, many courts have held that fees charged to students are permissible. Currently, 34 states permit at least one type of student user fee. Other courts, however, have held that such charges violate state constitutional provisions. Fifteen states and the District of Columbia prohibit these charges (see Swanson & King, 1997; Hamm & Crosser, 1991).

The legality of student user fees most often turns on whether the service or activity is an essential component of the education program. In general, fees charged for core instructional programs have been prohibited because such charges impede students' access to essential educational services. In contrast, fees charged for elective courses are common. Again, whether such fees are permitted is determined by the states' commitment to education as specified by the states' education clause. For example, although user fees for elective courses have been upheld in many states, California prohibits charges for any school-related activity (Swanson & King, 1997).

States also vary in their commitment to providing textbooks. For example, the following eight states permit user charges to be assessed for certain texts: Alaska, Illinois, Indiana, Iowa, Kansas, Kentucky, Utah, and Wisconsin (Hamm & Crosser, 1991). On the other hand, the majority of states disallows fees for textbooks or where permitted, requires financial assistance for economically disadvantaged students. It should be noted, however, that supplemental texts, such as workbooks, lab manuals, reference materials, and study guides, are often subject to user fees (Swanson & King, 1997).

Whereas instructional services and textbooks are often deemed an essential part of the educational program, in general, extracurricular activities, such as athletics, clubs, organizations, and field trips, have not been afforded this status. In 23 states, fees are permitted for participation in clubs and organizations, and 21 states permit fees for participation in interscholastic athletics (Hamm & Crosser, 1991).

Transportation fees have also been held by many state courts to be a nonessential part of schooling and therefore potentially subject to user fees. One might expect such fees to become prevalent as states move to offer children opportunities to exercise school choice options. Indeed, as students enroll in schools outside their local districts, payments to receiving districts will be required to offset differences in local tax collections.

Although student user fees for educational programs and services have been justified by the benefit standard, the use of these revenue streams raise several concerns. For instance, user fees often fail to take into consideration student (i.e., family) ability to pay. If so, these charges can function as a regressive tax. In other words, poorer households are required to pay a greater percentage of their income to meet these obligations than wealthier families. In response to this concern, some schools have established fee waivers to account for differences in household ability to pay. Absent fee waivers, students of poor families may be discouraged from participating in activities that require these fees (Swanson & King, 1997).

The potential to raise revenue from user fees needs to be viewed in light of the possibility that such charges will decrease student participation rates and place additional burdens on poor families. Schools and school districts that employ user fees should also be aware that the practice may strain parental-school relations. For example, it is possible that user fees may prompt negative responses from parents who view the charges as a form of double taxation. Indeed, parents subject to the fees may perceive that paying these charges in addition to their local property tax bill is akin to paying twice for education services.

Nonstudent User Fees

Schools may also raise revenues by selling or leasing services or facilities to private or community groups. In fact, there are a host of revenue-producing activities that schools engage in with businesses and community organizations. For example, it is common for schools to collect fees for the following (Swanson & King, 1997):

- Providing food preparation, data processing, accounting, and transportation services
- Leasing buildings to private groups, athletic fields to professional sports teams, and space to profit-making enterprises such as credit unions
- Instructional services for driver education, ceramics, carpentry, industrial arts, and swimming
- The sale of food service rights and vending machines

Schools have also begun to consider selling access to school property for commercial purposes. For example, in 1995-1996, the New York City School District implemented a plan to sell advertising space on school buses. The goal was to raise $5 million a year. Future plans include renting space for billboards and cellular relay antennas on school rooftops. Similar plans have been proposed in Seattle and Colorado Springs (see Cooper, 1996). Practices such as these clearly raise concerns with regard to perceived endorsement of school-advertised products.

School Partnerships

Schools and school districts often form partnerships with businesses and civic organizations to share operational, instructional,

and programmatic costs. For example, schools have formed coopera-
tive partnerships with government agencies for the following
purposes:

- Provide for the maintenance of grounds such as athletic fields
- Jointly use buildings for instruction
- Provide public vehicles and rail systems for transportation
- Share in the cost and use of community pools

Schools have also formed partnerships with community-based social service providers. For example, a California district offered
space to a family counseling center in exchange for services for the
student body. As demands on local education agencies to provide
these types of services grows, the ability of schools to develop partnerships with social service agencies will become increasingly important (Pijanowski & Monk, 1996).

Schools have also formed partnerships with colleges and universities. For example, a Massachusetts school district formed a partnership with Boston University to assist in implementing state-initiated
reforms. Beginning in 1989, the university agreed to manage the district for 10 years. School districts in New York have also entered into
relationships with the State University of New York to foster improvements in the instructional quality of their teachers and staff. In
fact, many colleges and universities form partnerships with local districts to create opportunities for professional development and to increase the pool of qualified college-bound students (see Swanson &
King, 1997).

School partnerships also offer businesses the opportunity to enter into schools and classrooms. Indeed, there are a host of examples
where business has sponsored school programs. School-business
partnerships are believed to yield benefits for all parties involved.
Schools benefit by gaining access to the expertise of business officials
who may then shape education programs to meet the future needs
of industry. Students benefit by being exposed to the demands of
tomorrow's labor market. Businesses benefit by gaining access to a
large audience and contributing to the education of future employees.

Perhaps the most noted school-business partnership is the one
formed between Whittle Communications Channel One and participating school districts. In exchange for programming and equip-

ment valued at $50,000 (e.g., satellite dish, two videotape recorders, and 19-inch networked televisions for classrooms with seating capacity of 25 or greater), students are exposed to a 12-minute news broadcast that contains 2 minutes of advertisements, usually in four 30-second blocks between the main news segments. In 1995, over 8 million students in approximately 12,000 schools received daily broadcasts from Channel One. This audience translates to approximately 40% of the students in 6th to 12th grades nationwide (Johnston, 1995).

Proponents of Channel One point to the modest gains in current-events knowledge among viewers and the development of a partnership between schools in search of revenue sources and businesses concerned about the education of youth. Critics point to the intrusion of the private sector into the curriculum and the perceived school endorsement of advertised products. As of 1992, the four states with the highest Channel One subscription rates were Michigan, Ohio, Pennsylvania, and Texas. In contrast, these services are banned in California, Massachusetts, New York, North Carolina, and Washington (Greenberg & Brand, 1993).

Channel One has taken a bold step in injecting corporate influence into schools. However, the practice is not new. For decades, businesses have gained access to students by offering teaching materials that serve to establish name recognition for products or companies. For example,

- "Without CFCs . . . life as we know it would be impossible." (Proctor and Gamble)
- "Coal is a good fuel choice" because protecting the environment is expensive. (American Coal Foundation)
- Nuclear waste is just as innocuous as the "leftovers" you get from making "scrambled eggs." (American Nuclear Society)

These examples represent only a few of the education packets available at one time or another to schools (see Lapp, 1994). More recently, a California school district raised revenues for schools by providing commercial access to students through advertising linked to homework assignments. The assignment required students to calculate the savings that could be realized by switching long-distance telephone carriers. In return, the district would receive a stipend for each household that changed to the sponsoring carrier (Pijanowski & Monk, 1996). Although these practices secure resources for school districts, it may be that these resource flows do not fully compensate children for the harmful effects of advertising directed at students.

Although schools and students represent a large market for the sale of goods or services, it is important to recognize that not all school-business partnerships are motivated by the desire to profit from future sales or to offset costs or secure revenues. In fact, many school-business partnerships have formed to address issues of organizational and administrative restructuring, operational efficiencies, and systemic reform. For example, partnership activities have stimulated and informed restructuring in the Los Angeles Unified School District. Similarly, business leaders have formed partnerships with New York City's schools to improve school programs (see Useem & Neild, 1995).

School partnerships have increased dramatically in the last decade, and so has their importance. In fact, the level of interaction with the community is often characteristic of districts that are successful in implementing school reforms. These may be formal relationships, such as the partnership between a university and a school district interested in teacher training programs. They may also be informal relationships, such as cases where a local business official advises school administrators on operational issues. In either case, it is becoming apparent that school improvement depends in large part on the interaction between schools and community groups.

Donations

Partnerships offer community groups the opportunity to interact and directly affect the educational programs of schools and districts on a continuing basis. Individuals and businesses not interested in developing such formal relationships may instead donate resources to schools for specific programs or activities. Donations come in a variety of forms. For example, donations may be in the form of cash or other negotiable instruments (e.g., stocks and bonds), or they may be made in the form of goods and services. Cash donations might be made to provide financial assistance to college-bound students. Noncash contributions, often called in-kind donations, have included computers, microscopes, lab equipment, automobiles, and full-service programs offered by private businesses or community groups. For example, private sponsorship of school programs include employment experiences for dropouts, artistic and cultural performances, and technology workshops for teachers, students, and administrators (Swanson & King, 1997).

In some cases, donations are made with restrictions as to their use. For example, cash may be donated with the provision that it only be used to purchase art supplies. This allows the donor control over how the resources will be expended. In this case, the donor is certain the gift will benefit the art department, rather than simply be pooled with other discretionary resources. It is important to keep in mind, however, that if existing funds are targeted for art supplies, these resources can be freed for use elsewhere.

The impact of in-kind donations on the pool of resources available to schools is difficult to measure. For example, how does one put a dollar figure on the value of a sponsored program or a 3-year-old computer? Although it is possible to estimate the cost of production or the fair market value of goods or services, often the task is difficult and imprecise. As a result, hard-to-value donations are often not reported by district officials as revenue sources.

On the other hand, cash donations are easy to measure. Much to the distress of school officials, however, corporate contributions to schools and school districts have averaged only between 3% and 5% of corporate giving (Swanson & King, 1997). This figure hardly suggests that corporate America has taken a proactive role in the education of the nation's youth. More troubling is the fact that the corporate downsizing of the 1990s and changes in federal tax policy may adversely affect corporate contributions to schools. For example, despite promises by corporate officials that increased profits would lead to increased giving, observers project that corporate charitable donations will remain relatively stagnant throughout the decade (Sommerfeld, 1995).

Educational Foundations

In response to recent declines in charitable giving, increasingly, districts are forming educational foundations to expand their revenue-raising capacities. Educational foundations are privately operated and financed, not-for-profit, tax-exempt entities organized to manage and promote giving from individuals and businesses. Educational foundations may be created to support all educational services or special programs only. For example, educational foundations have been established to raise money for the general operation of schools. Special project foundations have been formed to solicit funds for science laboratories, computer facilities, field trips, scholarship funds, and buildings.

Among the more popular target groups of educational foundations are alumni, employees, local businesses, and wealthy district residents. Once an individual or business is targeted, the foundation may employ a host of strategies to separate patrons from their money. Short-term development activities include telephone solicitations and organized fund-raisers (e.g., raffles, Bingo Nights). More aggressive development activities include assisting donors with estate planning. This strategy can be used to establish endowments that will produce future income streams or guarantee the district's inheritance of assets (e.g., land, art work; Swanson & King, 1997).

In recent years, there have been several noted examples of educational foundations that have benefited entire school systems. The I Have a Dream Foundation provides incentives to at-risk children in over 30 cities to complete school by ensuring future support for their higher education. The Minneapolis Five Percent Club exerts peer pressure on local businesses to encourage giving in the twin cities region. The MacArthur Foundation pledged $40 million to support Chicago's public schools (Swanson & King, 1997). The W. K. Kellogg Foundation is devoting $31 million to youth and education grants (Ferguson, 1996). Other examples include the following (see Bergholz, 1992; Leif, 1992; Useem & Neild, 1995):

- The Fund for New York City Public Education ($9.7 million)
- The Los Angeles Educational Partnership ($8.2 million)
- The Philadelphia Partnership for Education ($4 million)
- The San Francisco Education Fund
- The Washington Parents' Group Fund in Washington, D.C.
- The Allegheny Conference Fund in Pittsburgh, Pennsylvania

In addition, there are numerous examples of smaller school systems that have used foundations to secure sizable donations.[1]

Although educational foundations are separate entities, district officials should seek active advisory roles. In this capacity, the official should ensure that the activities of the foundation do not conflict with school policy or place the district in jeopardy of violating federal or state statutes. District officials should also caution foundation administrators from actions that adversely affect school-community relations. For example, charges of improprieties in the management of foundation funds could have a negative impact on the public's perception of district fiscal policy.[2]

Volunteer Services

The variety of services provided to districts in the form of donated time is a significant and often overlooked source of alternative revenues. In 1992, for example, a national survey indicated that over 16% of the respondents performed volunteer services to a school in the past year (Swanson & King, 1997). Indeed, volunteers can be found in school libraries, cafeterias, administrative offices, classrooms, gymnasiums, and supervising extracurricular activities. Volunteers are also instrumental in fund-raising activities. For example, Parent Teacher Associations (PTAs) sponsor raffles, carnivals, and promotional campaigns that facilitate the purchase of instructional supplies and equipment.

PTAs are not the only volunteer resource available to schools. In fact, although mothers, once the staple of parent volunteers, are entering the work force in growing numbers, schools have had success soliciting the senior population for volunteers. For example, DOVES (Dedicated Older Volunteers in Educational Service) coordinates volunteer activities in Springfield, Massachusetts, public schools (Swanson & King, 1997). Similarly, SMILES (Senior Motivators in Learning and Educational Services) is a nonprofit organization that mobilizes seniors to work in Salt Lake City's public schools. In 1992, the SMILES program provided 18,000 hours of volunteer time valued at $126,000 (Pijanowski & Monk, 1996).

Local booster clubs are perhaps the best known organization supported by volunteer efforts. Booster clubs (usually composed of parents) develop fund-raising strategies to support school activities of their choice. Booster club members can be found selling tickets, operating concession stands, and providing transportation to and from school-sponsored events. Booster club members also frequently coordinate with local vendors to provide donated or discounted supplies, such as uniforms, musical equipment, and lumber for the construction of theatrical sets. In addition to acting in a brokering capacity, booster clubs also sponsor fund-raising activities.

The thrust of volunteerism is the donation of time rather than money. In recent years, community volunteers have been encouraged to donate their expertise in areas that were once reserved for school personnel only. For example, district residents have actively participated in staff development programs. Corporations lend executives to advise districts on management practices or conduct performance audits (Swanson & King, 1997). And community members have participated in long-range planning to improve instructional quality and management efficiency. Perhaps the greatest gain realized from fostering volunteerism, however, is that it may viewed as part of a larger community-building exercise.

Investments of School Resources

Often, school districts receive large inflows of revenues, such as the proceeds of property tax collections, prior to the point in time when these resources must be expended for operating purposes. This temporary imbalance between current revenues and future expenses affords districts a window of opportunity to secure additional revenues through the investment of the resources on hand. In fact, good cash management policy dictates that district checking accounts should only maintain balances large enough to meet current expenses. All other resources should be pooled and invested to produce additional revenues.

The goals of good cash management include the following (Swanson & King, 1997):

- Safety: protecting the school district's resources against loss
- Liquidity: ability to convert investments into cash without penalties such as the loss of interest
- Yield: earning the maximum return on investments

Often, these goals are at odds. For example, a high return might be earned through a risky investment. It is the job of the school business official to balance these goals to provide safe, high-yield investments (see Nowakowski & Schneider, 1992).

Although state regulations often restrict the types of investments that can be made, district officials have several low-risk options available for investing temporary revenues. Among the more traditional investment options are the following:

- Savings accounts
- Money market accounts
- Certificates of deposit
- U.S. Treasury bills
- Investments in federal agency securities
- Repurchase agreements

Each of these investment options has advantages and disadvantages. For example, savings accounts earn interest daily, and withdrawals do not require prior notification. However, savings accounts traditionally offer the lowest interest rates of the options listed. Money market accounts and certificates of deposit offer higher interest rates but are less flexible than savings accounts because of the limits on the number of withdrawals that can be made in a given period. Penalties for early withdrawal are often a sign of poor investment management strategies.

U.S. Treasury bills offer perhaps the lowest risk and greatest return on federal government investments. Treasury bills also offer the advantage in that they are readily traded in secondary investment markets. In other words, if a school district that has invested in Treasury bills experiences a cash shortfall, the investments may be sold to other investors prior to the maturity date. In contrast, investments in federal agency securities, such as the Federal National Mortgage Association (Fannie Mae), offer a higher yield than Treasury bills but are not readily marketable.

Repurchase agreements, often termed "repos," are arrangements between districts and local lending institutions, whereby the district agrees to purchase a Treasury bill or other government security and sell it back to the bank at a future date. Banks enter into these arrangements to meet short-term cash shortages of their own. Repurchase agreements offer school districts an opportunity to earn high returns for limited investment periods, sometimes as short as a single day or week. In one instance, an industrious school district business manager was able to finance the construction of two elementary schools solely on the revenues earned through repurchase agreements. The story goes that to maximize the term of each agreement, the business official would travel to the state capital and receive state aid funds in hand. This effort saved the 3 or 4 days it would take to process and deposit the revenues into the district accounts (Pijanowski & Monk, 1996).

The manner in which school officials manage their cash resources also implicates several nonfinancial goals. For example, good cash management can result in the development of relationships with the local financial community. More important, good cash management can instill confidence in taxpayers that the district is maximizing the revenues available by sound investment strategies.[3]

Final Comments

Clearly, the nontraditional revenue sources described here should not be viewed as categorically distinct. In fact, many of the efforts employed by school officials to secure alternative sources of revenues are used in conjunction with each other. For example, educational foundations are often staffed by volunteers and facilitate the formation of partnerships between schools and private enterprises. What should be gleaned from the discussion is that there is growing evidence that schools and school districts are enjoying significant albeit varying levels of success at tapping these alternative sources of revenue. Indeed, studies have reported that alternative sources of revenue account for 3% to 15% of budgeted revenues (e.g., Pijanowski & Monk, 1996). It is even possible that these studies underestimate the amount of revenue derived from alternative sources due to their inability to place a dollar value on in-kind donations and volunteer services. Whereas schools and school districts that receive greater than 10% of total revenues from alternative sources may be atypical, they demonstrate the ability of these educational units to take full advantage of the revenue streams available to them.

Notes

1. For a comprehensive guide to educational foundations, see Jacqueline Ferguson's (1995) *The Education Grantseeker's Guide to Foundation and Corporate Funding.*

2. For an informative discussion of the use of educational foundations, readers may refer to "Partnerships and Education" in a special edition of the 1992 *Teachers College Record*, Ellen Condliffe Lagemann, ed., 93(3).

3. For further insight into the policies and procedures that govern cash management, readers can refer to Frederick Dembowski's (1986) "Cash Management," in G. C. Hentschke, *School Business Management: A Comparative Perspective.*

RECOMMENDATIONS FOR GENERATING SCHOOL REVENUES

Throughout the book, we have refrained from offering advice about what should be done by policymakers about raising revenue for the public schools. Instead, we have been content to explain the evaluative frameworks that are available and to report on the practices in various states and jurisdictions. Our presumption is that this kind of information is the most useful for policymakers at both state and local levels as they administer and seek to improve the existing school finance system.

However, it is hard to look this carefully at the revenue side of school finance and not form points of view about what appear to be the most promising directions for future public policy. In closing, we offer a few of these views not so much because we are convinced of their merit but more because we hope we can stimulate some serious debate about possible reforms that might otherwise be obscured.

In short, we see merit in developing a 4-point program that builds on the strengths of the existing system. Specifically, we encourage policymakers in these directions:

1. Work toward maintaining balance across the various available tax instruments. One of the virtues of the mixed school finance system that we rely on in the United States is that various tax instruments are used to generate revenues for the schools. No single tax instrument is perfect, and a viable strategy for balancing burdens involves reliance on a balanced set of instruments.

2. Recognize the merit of the property tax and work hard to reform its administration to comply with well-established principles of good government. Specifically, this involves developing a clear standard of value, relying on relatively large taxing jurisdictions (county level or larger), providing high levels of professional training and supervision for assessors, insisting on regular and frequent revaluation programs, and levying the tax in a manner that is easily understood by taxpayers.

3. Increase the amount of attention given to significant reforms of the property tax. Particularly promising reforms include the shift of commercial and other nonresidential parcels to regional levels and the use of equity-enhancing devices, such as circuit breakers and reverse-equity mortgages to lessen burdens on persons with low levels of income.

4. Begin careful experimentation with nontraditional revenue sources for the public schools.

On balance, we are optimistic about the prospects for raising necessary educational revenues in the United States as we approach the 21st century. The advent of new data collection and analysis capabilities promises to enhance the ability to fine tune revenue systems so that burdens are more equitably distributed. It is clear that these capabilities will develop. It is less clear that we will possess the political resolve to take full advantage of the new tools that are becoming available. Our collective resolve to provide appropriate fiscal support for the public schools will be tested in the years to come. We hope this volume helps to build a knowledge base that will allow us to meet this test.

REFERENCES

Abbott v. Burke, 100 N.J. 269, 495 A. 2d 376 (1985).

Advisory Commission on Intergovernmental Relations. (1994). *Significant Features of Fiscal Federalism, Vol. 1-2*. Washington, DC: Author.

Advisory Commission on Intergovernmental Relations. (1995). *Tax and Expenditure Limits on Local Governments*. Washington, DC: Author.

Bergholz, D. (1992). The public education fund. *Teachers College Record, 93*(3), 516-522.

Berne, R., & Netzer, D. (1995). Discrepancies between ideal characteristics of a property tax system and current practices in New York. *Journal of Education Finance, 21*(1), 39-56.

Blum, W. J., & Klaven, H., Jr. (1953). *The uneasy case for progressive taxation*. Chicago: University of Chicago Press.

Borg, M. O., Mason, P. M., & Shapiro, S. L. (1991). *The economic consequences of state lotteries*. New York: Praeger.

Census of Governments. (1982). *Taxable Property Values*, Bureau of Census (GC82-[2]). Washington, DC: Government Printing Office.

Census of Governments. (1994). *Taxable Property Values*, Bureau of Census (GC82-[2]-1). Washington, DC: Government Printing Office.

Center for the Study of States. (1995). *Public school finance programs of the United States and Canada 1990-91*. Albany: State University of New York, Nelson A. Rockefeller Institute of Government.

Clark, C. (1995). Regional school taxing units: The Texas experience. *Journal of Education Finance, 21*(1), 87-102.

Cooper, T. (1996). Buses and advertising: A unique way to raise funds. *School Business Affairs, 62*(7), 31-34.

Dembowski, F. (1986). Cash management. In G. C. Hentschke (Ed.), *School business management: A comparative perspective* (pp. 214-245). Berkeley: McCutchan.

Dembowski, F., & Kemmerer, F. (1984). An expanded tax base approach to wealth neutrality. *Journal of Education Finance, 9,* 474-484.

Dye, R. F., & Mcguire, T. J. (1992). Growth and variability of state individual income and general sales taxes. *National Tax Journal, 10*(4), 55-66.

Ferguson, J. (1996). The nature of private sector funding. *School Business Affairs, 62*(7), 11-24.

Gold, S. (1994). *Tax options for states needing more school revenues.* Report prepared for the National Education Association. West Haven, CT.

Greenberg, B., & Brand, J. (1993). Television news and advertising in schools: The Channel One controversy. *Journal of Communication, 43*(1), 143-151.

Hamm, R. W., & Crosser, S. (1991, June). School fees: Whatever happened to the notion of a free public education? *American School Board Journal, 178,* 29-31.

International Association of Assessing Officers. (1990). *Property appraisal and assessment administration.* Chicago: IAAO Publications.

Johnston, J. (1995). Channel One: The dilemma of teaching and selling. *Phi Delta Kappan, 2,* 437-442.

Jones, T. H., & Amalfitano, J. L. (1994). *America's gamble: Public school finance and state lotteries.* Lancaster, PA: Technomic.

Kearney, C. P. (1995). Reducing local school property taxes: Recent experience in Michigan. *Journal of Education Finance, 21*(1), 165-185.

Kroft, J. (1995). Varied paths to public relations. *Assessment Journal, 2* (2), 60-61.

Ladd, H. F. (1976). State-wide taxation of commercial and industrial property for education. *National Tax Journal, 29,* 143-153.

Ladd, H. F. (1992). Mimicking of local tax burdens among neighboring counties. *Public Finance Quarterly, 26*(4), 450-467.

Ladd, H. F., & Bradbury, K. L. (1988). City taxes and property tax bases. *National Tax Journal, 41*(4), 503-523.

Ladd, H. F., & Harris, E. W. (1995). Statewide taxation of nonresidential property for education. *Journal of Education Finance, 21*(1), 39-56.

Ladd, H. F., & Wilson, J. B. (1985). Education and tax limitations: Evidence from Massachusetts. *Journal of Education Finance, 10,* 281-296.

Lamitie, R. E., Glasheen, R. J., & Bentley, F. (1981). *Report of the expanded tax base study.* Albany: University of the State of New York.

Lankford, H., & Wyckoff, J. (1995). Property taxation, tax burden, and local educational finance in New York. *Journal of Education Finance, 21*(1), 57-86.

Leif, B. (1992). A New York City case study: The private sector and the reform of public education. *Teachers College Record, 93*(3), 524-535.

Lapp, D. (1994, Spring). Private gain, public loss. *Environmental Action, 26,* 14-17.

Mikesell, J. L. (1986). *Fiscal administration: Analysis and application for the public sector.* Homewood, IL: Dorsey.

Mikesell, J. L (1989). A note on the changing incidence of state lottery finance. *Social Science Quarterly, 70*(2), 513-520.

Mikesell, J. L., & Zorn, K. C. (1986). State lotteries as fiscal savior or state fraud: A look at the evidence. *Public Administration Review,* 311-319.

Monk, D. H. (1990). *Educational finance: An economic approach.* New York: McGraw-Hill.

Monk, D. H. (1995). Raising revenues for New York's public schools. A synthesis of options for policy makers. *Journal of Education Finance, 21* (11) 3-37.

Monk, D. H., & Haller, E. J. (1986). *Organizational alternatives for small rural schools.* Ithaca, NY: Cornell University.

Mullen, J. K. (1990). Property tax exemptions and local fiscal stress. *National Tax Journal, 43*(4), 467-479.

Nowakowski, B. C., & Schneider, R. (1992). A good business manager can save you money. *School Business Affairs, 62*(7), 43-51.

Odden, A., & Picus, L. (1992). *School finance: A policy perspective.* New York: McGraw-Hill.

Partnerships and education [Special issue]. (1992). *Teachers College Record, 93*(3).

Pechman, J. A. (1985). *Who paid the taxes, 1966-85?* Washington, DC: The Brookings Institute.

Pechman, J. A. (1986). *The rich, the poor, and the taxes they pay.* Washington, DC: Brookings Institute.

Picus, L. (1991). Cadillacs or Chevrolets? The evolution of state control over school finance in California. *Journal of Education Finance, 17,* 33-59.

Pijanowski, J. C., & Monk, D. H. (1996). Alternative school revenue sources: There are many fish in the sea. *School Business Affairs, 62*(7), 4-10.

Rosen, H. S. (1992). *Public finance.* Boston: Irwin.

Scholen, K. (1992). *Retirement income on the house,* Marshall: NCHEC.

Sommerfeld, M. (1995). Corporate giving expected to increase 3 percent this year. *Education Week, 15, 7.*

Stark, K. J. (1992). Rethinking statewide taxation of non-residential property for public schools. *The Yale Law Journal, 102,* 805-834.

State Board of Equalization and Assessment. (1992). *Local option property tax exemptions in New York State.* Albany, NY: Author.

Strauss, R. P. (1995). Reducing New York's reliance on the school property tax. *Journal of Education Finance, 21*(1), 123-164.

Swanson, A. D., & King, R. A. (1997). *School finance: Its economics and politics.* New York: Longman.

Useem, E. L., & Neild, R. C. (1995). A place at the table: The changing role of urban education funds. *Urban Education, 30,* 175-194.

Venti, S. F., & Wise, D. A. (1991). Aging and the income value of housing wealth. *Journal of Public Economics, 44,* 371-397.

Wildasin, D. (1987). The demand for public goods in the presence of tax exporting. *National Tax Journal, 40*(4), 591-601

Wyckoff, J. (1992). To what extent is education a public good? In E. Brown & R. L. Moore (Eds.), *Readings, issues, and problems in public finance* (pp. 6-11). Homewood, IL: Irwin.

Youngman, J. (1995). *Legal issues in property valuation and taxation: Cases and materials.* Chicago: IAAO Publications.

INDEX

Utah (*continued*)
  school revenue from state
    sources, 7
  tax limits on local school districts
    in, 78
  text book fees in, 122
  type of taxing jurisdiction in, 47
Utility, 25

Valuation, real property:
  farmland, 49-50
  large business property, 48-49
  residential homes, 48
  small business property, 48
  utility/railroad property, 49
Valuation methods, real property, 48.
  See also Capitalization of net
  income; Fair market value;
  Replacement cost less
  depreciation
Venti, S. F., 94
Vermont, 75
  assessed value of taxable property
    in, 45
  benefit use provision, 53
  circuit breaker programs, 90
  expenditure limits on local school
    districts in, 78
  homestead exemptions/credits, 72
  income tax rate, 23
  local property tax bases, 43
  reassessment period in, 64
  residential property legal standard
    of value, 56
  sales taxes, 29
  school revenue from federal
    sources, 7
  school revenue from local
    sources, 7
  school revenue from state
    sources, 7
  tax limits on local school districts
    in, 78
  type of taxing jurisdiction in, 47
Vertical equity, 9, 10, 15-16
Virginia:
  assessed value of taxable property
    in, 45
  benefit use provision, 53
  expenditure limits on local school
    districts in, 78

  homestead exemptions/credits, 73
  income tax rate, 23
  local property tax bases, 43
  reassessment period in, 64
  residential property legal standard
    of value, 56
  sales taxes, 29
  school revenue from federal
    sources, 7
  school revenue from local
    sources, 7
  school revenue from state
    sources, 7
  tax limits on local school districts
    in, 78
  type of taxing jurisdiction in, 47
Volunteer services, 120, 129-130
  as significant alternative revenue
    source, 129
  lending professional expertise, 130
  local booster clubs, 129-130
  Parent Teacher Association (PTAs),
    129
  senior citizens providing, 129

W. K. Kellogg Foundation, 128
Washington:
  assessed value of taxable property
    in, 45
  benefit use provision, 53
  expenditure limits on local school
    districts in, 78
  homestead exemptions/credits, 73
  income tax rate, 23, 26
  local property tax bases, 43
  reassessment period in, 64
  residential property legal standard
    of value, 56
  sales taxes, 29
  school revenue from federal
    sources, 7
  school revenue from local
    sources, 7
  school revenue from state
    sources, 7
  tax limits on local school districts
    in, 78
  type of taxing jurisdiction in, 47
Washington Parent's Group Fund
  (District of Columbia), 128
"Welcome neighbor" tax, 58

CORWIN
PRESS

The Corwin Press logo—a raven striding across an open book—represents the happy union of courage and learning. We are a professional-level publisher of books and journals for K–12 educators, and we are committed to creating and providing resources that embody these qualities. Corwin's motto is "Success for All Learners."